Heaven ♥n Earth©

GOD in a backpack

is **dedicated** to

my

Holy Spirit

who guides me
in all ways.

Thank you!

My

SOUL

is eternally grateful.

Table of Contents

Note to Readers

In this book, you will find God referred to as He. God, of course, is beyond gender, and the male pronoun is merely used for literary purposes.

Thank you for seeing God in the **omnipresence** of love where nothing and no one is excluded, not even a blade of grass! From such a place of inclusiveness, I would like to express how glad and honored I am that you are a part of this literary journey.

Perhaps we may meet on a trail one day—sharing the wonders and awe of the great outdoors—where things of truth are observable. When we touch a flower, we touch God. Dipping our toes into a river, we become aware of an eternal flow. Looking at a bright blue sky, we realize something bigger than us created our endless horizons.

We bump into God wherever we go!
I cannot wait to bump into you next.

PS: To not delay our adventure any further, grab your trail shoes! We are off to the woods any minute now.

FOREWORD

My personal experience backpacking.

New Zealand is responsible for my infatuation with backpacking. It is the perfect environment—with lots of nature and more sheep than people—where trails and solitude abound.

Since then, I have backpacked all over the globe, in Thailand, Borneo, Peru, Bolivia, the USA, Canada, Spain, and Switzerland. Vivid memories linger forever … the trek to Machu Picchu in Peru. Fabulous trails in the USA: the Appalachian Trail from Georgia to Maine (1700mi in 5 months); the John Muir Trail in the Sierra Nevada of California (200mi in 17 days) summiting Mt. Whitney; the Wonderland Trail around Mt. Rainier in Washington State (95mi in 10 days); the Na Pali coast of Kauai in Hawaii (22mi in 1 day); and great sections of the Pacific Crest and Continental Divide Trail. In Canada: the rugged West Coast Trail (75km in 5 days). In Europe: the Camino of Spain (888km in 26 days) and the breathtaking Alps of Switzerland (600km in 6 weeks, 5 days). Every year new trails await!

The exhilaration and beauty, the stillness and awe, are out of this world.
I walk in constant gratitude. Backpacking is an intimate experience between the elements, God, and I.
The great silence of the outdoors speaks volumes without words.

On solo trips, nobody but God is listening. He is "the one" calming my mind, regulating my heartbeat, finding my next water source, and sustaining me beyond what I think is my limit. He sees me through scary bear visits at night and is right by my side as a grizzly wanders my way—or an enormous male moose stares me down in a nearby water pond—or just as I fall hip-deep into a crevasse. Such internal pictures are etched into my heart forever. Nature at its best rubbing shoulders with me! What a privilege to be the observer from a safe distance.

What is most fascinating about backpacking is the fact that *the best adventures* happen with *the least gear.* With a small backpack, life becomes an absolute wonder. There are certainly hardships involved, especially when the weather is foul, but the simplicity of life brings out the best in me. Like a child, I look at everything with glee. Backpacking increases the appreciation of home conveniences, such as a bathroom and a kitchen. At home, I do not have to dig a hole in the ground, and my pantry is always full. When hiking, I am constantly hungry, and a simple ramen noodle soup tastes absolutely delicious! I usually bring my bear container (for safe food storage), which means extra weight. This inconvenience, however, saves me the hassle of hanging my food from a tree limb (to keep it out of reach from critters) … an acrobatic exercise I do not have the energy for at night when I just want to crash into oblivion to stretch out my tired and aching body. Oh, how I savor lying flat on my back after miles and miles on the trail the minute I put my pack down!

These few personal trail accounts may give you a glimpse of real-life experiences in the backcountry.
GOD in a backpack will paint you an even broader realistic picture of being exposed to beloved Mother Nature with nothing more than a pack on your back.

Backpacking adventures mirror in many ways *spiritual experiences* in life, which can be every bit as adventurous! Both impress our souls and are deeply transforming.

May this book move you in the direction of your own personal transformation.
Suspense and adventure await you!

INTRODUCTION

Welcome, dear Readers!

This is your **instruction manual** to heaven.
God will be part of the expedition and ride along in your backpack.
Do not fret; He is lighter than you think!

Are you ready to embrace this great (and seemingly impossible) paradox?
Your YES will propel you into a life of wonders.

OK, let's get packing!

Complexity meets Simplicity

How can our big
GOD
possibly fit into a small little backpack?
Why even attempt to do so?

Truth be told, I refuse to leave home without Him. With Him in my pack, I feel safe.
As to size, you will be surprised how pliable He is!

Part I   **GOD in a backpack**

Trip details

Destination	:	The **Kingdom of Heaven**
Length of trip	:	**0 miles** (without counting the unnecessary detours)
Level of difficulty	:	**easy** (once you know who you are)
Gear	:	**unusual** (pack as instructed)

Compressing items into a pack is one thing. Compressing **God** into a pack is an entirely different matter!

As complex as God appears, He is so humble in His greatness that He does not mind being compressed. Nothing hurts Him. He is extremely flexible, and you cannot possibly break Him. God is not heavy like everybody assumes. On the contrary, He is as light as a feather!

What started as a typical challenge of bringing the 10 Essentials for survival (according to mountaineering rules) soon evolved into a spiritual lesson about the **true laws** of life.

Earlier packing attempts revealed that regular Essentials such as an emergency kit, a fire starter, extra food, rain gear, etc. were not suitable for a trip to the Kingdom of Heaven. We needed something lighter and more durable. Our **new set** of Essentials had to be foolproof in its reliability, withstand the wear and tear, and last the distance—as all of humanity depends on it for survival—now and in the future!

What came to our rescue (in our packing frenzy) was the sudden realization that the most outrageous goal can be easily achieved when God is on our side. To have Him on board is our saving grace! God Himself volunteered as our mentor once it came down to the final selection process of what to pack. Under His advice, we decided on the following 10 Essentials: **LOVE, JOY, TRUTH, FREEDOM, RESPONSIBILITY, WISDOM, FORGIVENESS, HUMOR, ART,** and **SIMPLICITY**. Actually, it was SIMPLICITY making all of our (last-minute) packing choices, whom God put in charge, to ensure our loads stay light! It is simply the expert in such matters.

Ever since we bravely embraced our destiny, the Kingdom of Heaven, God rewarded us with personal wisdom, and **_inner knowing_** became our new route finder. We could comfortably ditch our GPS (among many other things) and happily press on to unknown horizons. But wait a minute, we still have some packing to do!

Dear Readers, enough said, the sign-up sheet is in front of you. You can decide today to become participants in **_a life of truth_**. The backpacking trip is a mere preparation exercise in that direction.

Are you keen to experience life as **_grace_** and **_ease_**?
Are you ready to embrace a life of **_heaven_** on **_earth_**?

YOU are the ones deciding on the day of your **_freedom_**.
YOU are the ultimate authority concerning the **_quality_** of your life.

Free will gives you the power of **_personal direction_**.
Make **_delight_** your daily choice!

Below is your pack list.
Bring your **10 Essentials**—they are your life line!

The following chapters will give you details on the nature of each Essential. We briefly discuss the location of purchase, cost, weight, and <u>how and where</u> to pack them. Once you have carefully fit them all in, we will check the base weight of your pack and decide what other items of personal choice you may afford to add.

Essential no. 1	**LOVE**
Essential no. 2	**JOY**
Essential no. 3	**TRUTH**
Essential no. 4	**FREEDOM**
Essential no. 5	**RESPONSIBILITY**
Essential no. 6	**WISDOM**
Essential no. 7	**FORGIVENESS**
Essential no. 8	**HUMOR**
Essential no. 9	**ART**
Essential no. 10	**SIMPLICITY**

Happy trails !

Essential no. 1		LOVE

Where to purchase	:	within your sacred heart, the throne of your soul
Cost	:	$ 0.00—and daily application
Weight	:	0.00 lbs—**LOVE** is as light as it is rich
Where to pack	:	anywhere, leave room for JOY next to it

LOVE is the Mother of all Essentials.

If we were allowed to bring one Essential only, it would most definitely be **LOVE**. Our nine others we primarily pack for good company, but **LOVE** is their very source.

LOVE is the "wool of our sweater" keeping us warm and fuzzy, whereas the other Essentials are the various patterns and color strands, accentuating and enhancing the overall fabric of **LOVE**. Wool has the advantage of being water-resistant in bad weather (an important detail when backpacking).

With **LOVE** in our packs, we feel prepared. Only the best equipment will do, with a destination of such far-reaching horizons!

To get off on the right foot, we will start by shedding light on our 1st Essential, finding out together ...

what **LOVE** is   and   what it is _not_.

If God had a name, it would surely be **LOVE**.
LOVE is the umbrella term and underlying reason for our vast and magnificent existence.

Even though **LOVE** can be _blocked_, _ignored_, or _overshadowed_, we can never, under any circumstance, make it _disappear_. That is an impossibility! We cannot _un-create_ what God created and what God Himself is. No matter how destructive we choose to be, **LOVE** is never going to be _eradicated_.

This is really good news, for starters!

God gave us free will: to _**accept**_ or _**deny**_ our true nature and to learn from the consequence of our choice. As His children, we are naturally **LOVE** and here on earth to discover that for ourselves. This planet is our inheritance and playground to prove ourselves as capable co-creators for the benefit and enjoyment of all. _Denying_ we are **LOVE** and _turning away_ from our Creator (and supplier of energy) provokes such unbearable hardships in life that we are forced to reconsider our actions. Downtrodden, we are more ready than ever to surrender to God's will, which is nothing other than **LOVE** and kindness. Once we humbly admit our foolishness of _dis-connecting_ from our source, we gladly embrace a new choice: to _**accept**_ and _**extend**_ **LOVE**, which is by far more rewarding. This reorientation will naturally bring us HOME. By recognizing ourselves _as_ **LOVE**, we have found a reliable compass for life!

With this new recognition of TRUTH, we become capable leaders on the path.

We can now effectively help others on the journey of self-discovery. As a team, we safely trek over hills and mountains, finding our inner strength. By daring the outdoors, we are putting ourselves and God to the test while testing our equipment for durability.

Will it hold up? How much space will it take up in our packs? Can we afford to bring **LOVE**?
Is it ... too heavy? ... too bulky? ... too pricey? ... or just wishful thinking?

The wondrous thing about **LOVE**, there is no weight to it, nor does it take up any space.

Exciting facts, indeed!

LOVE being our very nature travels *with* us wherever we go, without adding an ounce to our gear. By simply *being* **LOVE**, we will have already packed the most important Essential, ensuring a successful trip to the furthest destination in the history of humankind! What a revolutionary concept. Too good to be true?

Dear Readers, before your valued answer (to yourself) I would like to pose a sincere question:
Can you **accept** the best-case scenario to be **easy**, **simple**, and **free**?

The TRUTH is such a reversal of circumstance—it stands in gaping contrast to what the world has become used to and the *lies* it has accepted for so long ...
that everything desirable should be *difficult, impossible,* and *expensive*?

This brings us to the question of price. Amazingly so, **LOVE** costs nothing (true **LOVE**, that is). It is not a *thing* but a *quality* of being. We are born with it! Digest this simple TRUTH, and stash it away in your heart as the most special treasure to behold. YOU are that very treasure called **LOVE**.

To introduce a refreshingly "new and true" concept and to counterbalance the "hum-drum" of worldly living, we have made up our minds to try something entirely different for a change:
On *our* trip, we are going to achieve great things with a **light heart**. We will pack **ultra-light** (since anything heavy has never been known to add any benefits). We will remain **open** (**LOVE**'s natural stance) and assure each other ahead of time that **all** will be arriving safe and sound at our precious destination ...

the Kingdom of Heaven.

How can we be so sure?   **LOVE** knows the way HOME.

Get ready to embark upon a most worthwhile adventure and pure celebration of life! To keep up the good cheer, we chant as we prep:

LOVE... here I come... with YOU as my guide... with YOU at my side!

Why did I wait so long to choose YOU as my steady companion?
God only knows.

AMEN

Personal notes:

1) What is your understanding of the chapter? List three key elements.
2) What is your personal interpretation of **LOVE**?
3) What aspects of **LOVE** have you discovered within yourself?
4) What aspects of **LOVE** would you like to cultivate or unearth?
5) What is your approach to making that happen?

Thank you for sharing your insights and inspiration!

Essential no. 2   JOY

Where to purchase	:	**JOY** is not for sale; it is a product of LOVE
Cost	:	$ 0.00—and lots of loving
Weight	:	0.00 lbs—**JOY** carries you on the wings of laughter
Where to pack	:	wherever you pack LOVE, there is **JOY**

JOY is your reward for right living. What is right living? To LOVE.

Our 2nd Essential, **JOY**, is extremely dear to us. How so? It skips and hops along the trail, is lighthearted, smiles a lot, does somersaults, and giggles uncontrollably at times. Our spirit is instantly lifted in its presence! Everybody loves **JOY**. Where it shows up, it gets immediately noticed, and people are naturally drawn to it. Its bubbly nature is contagious. **JOY** brings color and sunshine to a room and lights up the darkest of forests. It is also very attractive. There are so many attributes to **JOY**, it would take a lifetime to enumerate them all.

Today, we are going to dig up the TRUTH ... to find **JOY**'s precious *source*.
Take out your shovels! Consider it your trail maintenance day.

   Like a tree has roots, **JOY** is rooted in LOVE.
LOVE is the source of **JOY**.

What a discovery! That was well worth your sweat, was it not? Everybody wants **JOY**, but rarely do people know how to make it their constant companion. Having unearthed the TRUTH yourself, you now know, it takes LOVE for **JOY** to be present.

JOY follows LOVE like a dog follows a scent. They are inseparable! That is a huge secret to remember.

Here's a simple recipe to ease your journey	:	stop chasing **JOY**—be LOVE—and you **have** them **both**!
People typically think	:	to **have** something—they must **do** something.
But the TRUTH is	:	**be** what you want to **have**—and it will **come to you**!

LOVE is a magnet, remember? It draws **JOY** powerfully unto itself. LOVE and **JOY** are forever intertwined and part of *your* heavenly genetics. Ponder that wonder for a minute. That wonder is you!

You might ask yourself: If I am such a wonder, why does life look bleak sometimes, and why do I not feel joyous every day? Life is one giant test of LOVE. **JOY** eludes us if we do *not* operate with LOVE. The more we LOVE, the more joyous life is! As earthlings on the path of evolution, we tend to *look* for **JOY** instead of allowing it to bubble up from within. We erroneously hope to find it in substitutes such as alcohol, sex, drugs, power, control, or wealth where it can never be found. **JOY** needn't be chased or obtained—it is a gift of LOVE.

Important to realize is that ALL our cravings have ONE underlying reason. It is our craving for LOVE. Once we know we **are** LOVE, the chase is over! Now, LOVE stills our hunger and fulfills our soul, and we can finally break *free* from our addictions. Never look for LOVE or **JOY** *outside* of yourself. **JOY** is generated from *within* your loving self.

What is the actual hold-up of experiencing **JOY** right now? Only *mis*perception. We see ourselves as smaller and more insignificant than what we are in reality. We are 100% LOVE! The price for *not* knowing self is huge. It puts us on a downward spiral of addictive behavior, luring us into substitutes that are less than satisfying.

Only LOVE truly satisfies, and it comes with JOY on its heels!

How exactly do we generate **JOY**? LOVE plenty and your cup of **JOY** will ... runneth over ... This is your cliff note for the trail. Stick it in the top pouch of your pack for quick access as a valuable reminder.

Our long-term goal is to accumulate as much **JOY** as life offers time. Our short-term goal is to prep for this backpacking trip, which is the perfect springboard to successfully resolve all of our challenges. Why do we have challenges in the first place? As humans, we are still in training to fully understand the laws of life. This book helps us jog our memory of how to live life with grace rather than strive. We learn to lean on God and lean on LOVE for everything. Once we realize we **are** LOVE, problems vanish quickly!

This realization helps us avoid the snares and traps of life. Anything *isolated* or *separated* from LOVE is a snare. Sex without LOVE is a trap, making people feel lonely and abused. Greed that *chases* wealth and obtains power and control through force (instead of LOVE) leads to other unhappy dead-ends. Drugs and alcoholism are addictive escapades, numbing the pain, never filling the void (of LOVE). Rely on the GPS of your heart instead! While trekking through some dark valleys (of life), take LOVE as your compass and imagine it to be your true North. Follow it unerringly! True LOVE will navigate you safely to our destination, the Kingdom of Heaven, evoking real and *lasting* **JOY**.

As you carefully prep and learn how to pack your backpack, the 10 Essentials become second nature. By the time you are done packing, you will have fully absorbed them into your bloodstream :)

As a quick summary, some practical tips for you to take HOME: How do you become **JOY** today?

1) LOVE. If you feel empty and would rather *be* loved ... know ... God loves you every second. Drink it in!
2) Stop desiring **JOY**. Simply LOVE. You will experience **JOY** as a natural consequence.
3) Give **JOY** a hug. It has been waiting for your embrace. Compassionate human touch is soothing.
4) Share **JOY** with whomever you meet. You will be a happy camper indeed. Watch **JOY** multiply.

Now that you are beaming with JOY, I would like to say: Thank you for shining your light!
You are simply radiant.

AMEN

Personal notes:

1) What is your understanding of the chapter? List three key elements.
2) What is your personal interpretation of **JOY**?
3) What aspects of **JOY** have you discovered within yourself?
4) What aspects of **JOY** would you like to cultivate or unearth?
5) What is your approach to making that happen?

Thank you for sharing your insights and inspiration!

Essential no. 3   TRUTH

Where to purchase	:	in the transparency of your heart
Cost	:	$ 0.00—and courage to truly *see* yourself
Weight	:	0.00 lbs—**TRUTH** makes the pack feel considerably lighter
Where to pack	:	tucked close to FORGIVENESS, sandwiched between FREEDOM

TRUTH is completely transparent.

Humorously, our 3rd Essential is so transparent that it is hard to find once packed. We have to make sure to go over our checklist not to leave town without it!

Where things notoriously take up too much space, **TRUTH** has a way of *creating space,* which is a pretty magical concept considering we are backpacking. Usually, a backpacker's greatest challenge is "how to fit" everything in. With **TRUTH**, we have no such problem. *Transparency* packs extremely light. This quickly makes it a backpacker's favorite.

What else does **TRUTH** offer besides *transparency* and *space? Clarity, lightness, freedom, consistency,* and *inclusiveness.* What an array of qualities! They greatly improve our chances of reaching our lofty goal.

TRUTH will make our trip so much easier by being the exact opposite of a burden. Take a deep breath, participants, as we have just lightened our loads! With the extra weight off of our backs and plenty of space, we are headed in the right direction. I do not see how anyone would object to bringing **TRUTH** along?

What made **TRUTH** so multi-faceted? Its many talents.

Have you noticed how talents always look *easy* when performed by professionals?

How can you become a "pro" at **TRUTH**? Emulate it every day.

It takes many repetitions to develop a particular talent and the right kind of coach. The best coach to hire is your heart (it knows how to be truthful). Internal inquiry cuts down on our costs significantly; any other coach would be quite an expense! Is it not surprising how little "money" is of value when it comes to the greatest values of all? **TRUTH** cannot be bought—it is wrought free—from the stronghold of deception. Practice **TRUTH** daily by looking inward before you go to sleep.

What would you ask your heart to *do* to become completely truthful?

Ask it for willingness to forgive all personal lies. If you do not know where your lies are, look at what you are hiding. If you think you have nothing to hide, search your heart whether you are ashamed of anything. Your heart will know. When it feels absolutely *carefree,* you are in the clear!

Clarity makes the day look bright. With **TRUTH**, life feels airy and light, and you are inwardly buoyant. Who does not want to be buoyant when backpacking? Imagine you are floating along while carrying your pack, and it is so very light that it practically lifts you up! This is the kind of *lightness* **TRUTH** brings.

How can **TRUTH** be measured?   By how consistent and inclusive it is.

God loves everybody the same, without exception and consistently so. His LOVE does not depend on creed, deed, or circumstance. That is the **TRUTH** to emulate and trust. Be *consistent* and *inclusive*. Be like the sun that rises every day (not just on some days) and shines on everybody (not just on a few special people). Any "exclusive" version of **TRUTH** is a warped derivative to suit a personal agenda. **TRUTH** does not have versions.

We were speaking of *transparency* earlier: Have you noticed, the more truthful you are, the *lighter* and more *transparent* you become? That is the beginning of ascension! **TRUTH** ascends like water evaporates. Lies stick to the muck.

As humans, we naturally *yearn* for heaven (because it is our origin). We search for it, we hope and dream … but seem incapable of finding it. Is it because we are looking out of eyes full of deceit and judgment? Once our eyes look inward, and we see nothing but **TRUTH** inside, our outward glance becomes as innocent and honest as *transparency* itself. Now, we no longer expect bad things to happen, and we no longer look for a single fault in anyone else. That is the day we *see* heaven all around us!
It takes *heaven* to see *heaven* and **TRUTH** to recognize **TRUTH**. We have to *be* it before we can *see* it.

Have you created *transparency, space, clarity, lightness, freedom, consistency,* and *inclusiveness* within yourself (yet)? If you are not done with the process, you are not done packing. Remember, it is a prerequisite to literally *become* all the Essentials before you are ready for the trip. To ease your soul, here's a small hint: Simply shed falseness and lay bare your **TRUTH**. Within, you find all the Essentials intact. *Becoming* is nothing more than a stripping of lies. Underneath, you are a wholesome and radiant child of God!

As far as the **TRUTH** is concerned, just keep shining your *inner* light into the deepest recesses of your being. Search for any shadows trying to obscure you. Boldly shine the light until all those little (or big) monsters take off running. They will quickly flee because they are afraid of the light!
The light of **TRUTH** *frees* you from the darkness. That is what is meant by "the **TRUTH** shall set you free."

Simply be willing to *look* at yourself. Look at the good *and* the bad, and the light will take care of the rest. Light is like OxiClean (a multi-purpose cleaning agent) that wipes out pernicious stains. The bad parts in us can only exist as long as we keep them hidden and in the dark. **TRUTH** takes courage, but once we bravely take the leap, it effectively kick-starts our FORGIVENESS process, which will naturally happen with our *willingness* to face the light.

It takes light to **see** what errors to forgive.

TRUTH is the best flashlight you ever had. No batteries required!
Here's a bumper sticker before heading "into the wild":

TRUTH is … where I allow LIGHT to enter …

AMEN

Personal notes:

1) What is your understanding of the chapter? List three key elements.
2) What is your personal interpretation of **TRUTH**?
3) What aspects of **TRUTH** have you discovered within yourself?
4) What aspects of **TRUTH** would you like to cultivate or unearth?
5) What is your approach to making that happen?

....
....
....
....
....
....
....
....
....
....
....
....
....
....
....
....
....
....
....
....
....
....
....
....
....
....
....
....
....
....
....
....

Thank you for sharing your insights and inspiration!

Essential no. 4		FREEDOM

Where to purchase	:	not for purchase, you are *born* free
Cost	:	$ 0.00—**FREEDOM** is a God given gift
Weight	:	0.00 lbs—**FREEDOM** is as light as air
Where to pack	:	for safety purposes, right next to RESPONSIBILITY

FREEDOM flows like a river, blessing the land wherever it touches.

Adventures reach it from the unknown. It trusts and is unbound. Many experiences come its way because it is *open*.

FREEDOM knows *no fear.*

It acts spontaneously and courageously.

Our 4th Essential is a champion at expressing its own nature. It is refreshingly bold and never holds back.

Where is **FREEDOM** located?

Primarily *within*, but it roams freely from there. **FREEDOM** is familiar with infinity and eternity. Heaven is its origin and destination—and everything in between—belongs to it as well.

FREEDOM depends on *allowance,* needs *understanding, respect,* and *recognition.*

Even though **FREEDOM** is our birthright, it is often abused or left dormant and is probably the most misunderstood of all Essentials.

We either tend to imprison ourselves (or others) because we do not trust ourselves with **FREEDOM,** or we obey a cultural imprint without question. Deep down, we yearn for **FREEDOM** but do not dare to see what is out there. Like caged birds, we are used to conforming to our prison walls. Have we noticed the door is *open*? Are we scared to take flight? The cage is not comfortable (... never was). It is confining but "feels safe" because it is the known.

FREEDOM lies beyond the fence of the known.

The unknown belongs to the realm of LOVE, which is fearless.

Once we remember we *are* LOVE, we will trust **FREEDOM** to guide us in the exploration of the unknown.

On our journey together, we discover the right and necessity to be ourselves (the only true way to be)! **FREEDOM** is our teacher of unbridled expression.

Unfortunately, there are many examples in the world where **FREEDOM** is restricted from the *outside*. Too often, however, we restrict ourselves from the *inside* when *not* subjected to other people's dictation.

Needless to say, **FREEDOM** often remains a beautiful *word* that desperately wants to be *lived*.

Very few people know how to live **FREEDOM** graciously. Some attain it, then squander it. Many snares seem to lay in wait to strangle our precious commodity called **FREEDOM**. In such instances, we can rely on the support of our other Essentials, who gladly rush to our aid in resurrecting **FREEDOM**.

FORGIVENESS heals the error of squandering **FREEDOM**. LOVE allows **FREEDOM** to be itself. TRUTH sets it free. WISDOM guides **FREEDOM** safely. RESPONSIBILITY maintains **FREEDOM** to ensure its continuance. To handle **FREEDOM** responsibly means you invite your conscience to make healthy decisions. Being free does not mean "I can do anything I want." Be wise to *remain* free! Make life-enhancing decisions to nurture **FREEDOM** and extend its lifespan.

With the 10 Essentials, we have a whole army acting in our best interest. No matter how diametrically opposed to God's intent humanity has wandered, there is eternal hope for sound recovery!

How can we start to live **FREEDOM** as God intended?

Signing up for this backpacking trip is a good start. Listen to what each Essential has to say. Together, we will *remember* who we are (LOVE), reclaim our inheritance as children of God, and live a marvelous life. Today, we simply decide to leave our (conditioned) forgetfulness behind!

Here are some profound realizations to recall our ancient memory:

* We *are* LOVE, therefore we *can* LOVE.
* To LOVE means to set *free*. What comes back by *free will* is ours forever.
* God set us *free* so we can learn everything about LOVE and life there is to learn.

Nature, where **FREEDOM** is on display every day, is the perfect setting for backpacking and offers ideal grounds for the understanding of life. Feel inspired by **FREEDOM** wherever you tread! You will see many rivers flow freely, painting a beautiful picture of allowance. Each waterdrop bursts with JOY as it jumps over hurdles without complaint or regret, demonstrating a **FREEDOM** of being and an acceptance of what is without the slightest hesitation, resistance, or fear. A plant is never jealous of another. It focuses on its own season to bloom, does not compare, and simply—is—its own splendor.

Looking to nature as our prime example of **FREEDOM**, I am sending you HOME with a mantra:

Allow yourself the FREEDOM ... to be your true and beautiful YOU.

AMEN

Personal notes:

1) What is your understanding of the chapter? List three key elements.
2) What is your personal interpretation of **FREEDOM**?
3) What aspects of **FREEDOM** have you discovered within yourself?
4) What aspects of **FREEDOM** would you like to cultivate or unearth?
5) What is your approach to making that happen?

....
....
....
....
....
....
....
....
....
....
....
....
....
....
....
....
....
....
....
....
....
....
....
....
....
....
....

Thank you for sharing your insights and inspiration!

Essential no. 5 RESPONSIBILITY

Where to purchase	:	in the depth of your conscience
Cost	:	$ 0.00—common sense and fairness
Weight	:	0.00 lbs—being irresponsible weighs heavily
Where to pack	:	right by FREEDOM, in the neighborhood of LOVE and TRUTH

RESPONSIBILITY is our 5th Essential, and without it, we are not leaving! This is your trip leader speaking.

Does this not sound a little radical?

It is not radical but rational. It would be irresponsible *not* to bring **RESPONSIBILITY** with us, especially now that we have packed FREEDOM. Do you think we are going to risk our dear friend? A friend like FREEDOM is hard to come by, and we are not going to lose someone special over irresponsible behavior.

OK, understood! But why be so uptight and serious all of a sudden?

I am not uptight, just cautious.

In my lifetime, I have seen too many people *yearn* for FREEDOM. And once they have it, they wreck it! That is a sad scenario, and I will not let that happen to us.

Why do people have such a hard time *handling* FREEDOM wisely?

Generally, people do not allow themselves *enough* FREEDOM. Deep down, they do not entirely trust themselves with it. When they finally break *free*, they are not very good at navigating it. In the beginning stages of enjoying newfound FREEDOM, people tend to go wild and end up going overboard.

That is where **RESPONSIBILITY** comes in. Pair the two up, and they will have a long and healthy life!

What **RESPONSIBILITY** does best is *maintain* FREEDOM and watch over it with loving care.

It measures how much FREEDOM is healthy to issue and moderates its intake. **RESPONSIBILITY** tells it when to go to bed, when to rise, <u>what to do</u> and <u>what *not* to do</u>, and it imparts common sense in general. Our 5th Essential can be quite a hard taskmaster. But over time, we all develop an appreciation for it. It skillfully keeps us on the "straight and narrow." Call it tough LOVE if you will. **RESPONSIBILITY** teaches us healthy discipline.

You may also liken it to a good parent who has to say NO at times, to protect the child from its own foolishness (such as running into the street or jumping off a cliff) until it becomes mature and wise enough *not* to hurt itself. **RESPONSIBILITY,** our cheapest life insurance, is willing to do all the "dirty work," and yet, it does not cost us a dime, which is amazing! TRUTH be told, being responsible and policing the environment is not exactly the most comfortable position to behold.

What happens once we arrive in the Kingdom of Heaven? Do we still need **RESPONSIBILITY**?

Nothing is *needed* in heaven, which is fully self-sustained through LOVE. However, what *makes* it to heaven will certainly be welcomed and celebrated. Only LOVE enters heaven! One could say, it is the *responsible aspect* of LOVE that allows it to enter.

RESPONSIBILITY is very necessary as long as we reside on earth. Its contribution to balance and survival is crucial—it keeps us oriented the right way and ensures longevity. **RESPONSIBILITY** takes charge of the formative character of life. It sets healthy limits, has a great sense of (inner and outer) direction, and handles whatever is in front of it without delay. It never beats around the bush, is clear spoken, and to the point. TRUTH is well familiar with it. **RESPONSIBILITY** knows right from wrong and works closely with a person's conscience. JOY celebrates **RESPONSIBILITY** for supporting FREEDOM in such a significant way!

LOVE certainly appreciates the fact we are bringing **RESPONSIBILITY** along. In its company, it will not have to deal with touchy moments alone. People tend to get very defensive when they are told what to do. **RESPONSIBILITY** steps in without wavering and takes care of sensitive situations. That is its task, and it does not mind. Taking charge lies in its nature. Like a police officer, it will protect you but can be *rough* when provoked, showing the person there are *consequences* to wrong behavior!

Do we realize how fortunate we are to have **RESPONSIBILITY** come on this trip with us? We will have no disciplinary issues, and our fellow hikers can count on an overseer, should they get too distracted or stray.

God, of course, is the one who invented **RESPONSIBILITY** and is pleased to see we have selected it as one of our Essentials! He created such a great universe, and with **RESPONSIBILITY** under our belt, He is assured we are taking good care of our earth and each other.

Where we choose to be careless, we mostly hurt ourselves, but we also affect others and our environment negatively. Our deliberate carelessness is responsible for our delay in reaching heaven. Start caring!
Why prolong suffering for ourselves and others?

RESPONSIBILITY means—to *respond* correctly rather than to *react* impulsively—which makes it a very worthy item on our pack list. You will never hear it say: "I don't care."

When it comes to trail maintenance, it teaches us *not* to litter. We shall only leave footprints behind, thank God! This deserves a moment of appreciation expressed out loud:
"**RESPONSIBILITY,** you are one of a kind! Thank you for looking out for us. We love you dearly."

Visibly encouraged, **RESPONSIBILITY** interlocks fingers with FREEDOM, and they walk hand in hand into ... paradise.

As a pair, they are sure to make it all the way to eternity!

AMEN

Personal notes:

1) What is your understanding of the chapter? List three key elements.
2) What is your personal interpretation of **RESPONSIBILITY**?
3) What aspects of **RESPONSIBILITY** have you discovered within yourself?
4) What aspects of **RESPONSIBILITY** would you like to cultivate or unearth?
5) What is your approach to making that happen?

Thank you for sharing your insights and inspiration!

Essential no. 6		WISDOM

Where to purchase	:	go within; **WISDOM** is stored in your soul
Cost	:	$ 0.00—courage and introspection
Weight	:	0.00 lbs—**WISDOM** is light; being unwise is a heavy load to carry
Where to pack	:	between FREEDOM and RESPONSIBILITY

How is **WISDOM** born?

It is either *imparted* by listening to the voice of God or *earned* through personal experiences that have undergone the process of reflection.

People more often than not choose the latter method because they are used to *earning* things the hard way rather than *accepting* God's grace.

This preference is part of our learning curve as humans until we are *wise* enough to remember we are *worthy* of God's gifts.

As we grow in **WISDOM,** we also grow in our capacity to *accept* our inheritance of the Kingdom of Heaven within.

That is the *vertical* approach of *receiving* **WISDOM,** which is instantaneous and effortless! This is how miracles are granted and how grace is imparted. It takes openness of the heart and stilling of the mind.

The *horizontal* approach of *earning* **WISDOM** happens through our life lessons on earth, offered in time and space. We glean **WISDOM** by processing our experiences and deriving understanding from them.

WISDOM is guaranteed, no matter the approach, as long as we demonstrate a sincere yearning. It is simply important to know that both methods exist. It takes a great accumulation of **WISDOM** before we allow *ease* in our lives.

Receiving **WISDOM** from heaven—as well as gleaning **WISDOM** through life—takes practice! Our trip preparations (and this book) offer wonderful opportunities to learn both modalities.

Looking at **WISDOM** in its totality reveals a true collage of life. **WISDOM** carries an aspect of all our Essentials *within*. It is our quilt for picnics. Shall we admire the various "pieces of fabric" for a minute to fully appreciate the artwork?

WISDOM requires a lot of LOVE to be courageous enough to engage in a multitude of experiences. RESPONSIBILITY is needed to handle and maintain FREEDOM, offering a playground to grow wise.

TRUTH is necessary to make an honest analysis and derive **WISDOM**. Without FORGIVENESS, we can never become wise enough *not* to make mistakes. The ART of life advises us to apply SIMPLICITY and HUMOR in every circumstance. JOY brings the preciousness of living to the surface—all leading to **WISDOM** eventually!

This hodge-podge of characteristics makes **WISDOM** a very seasoned and mature Essential. It is a strong asset and utterly reliable. Everybody feels reassured and happy to count it among the valuable resources of our entire expedition team.

Its company is admired and treasured. **WISDOM** is sure-footed, tried and true, and makes a great hiking partner for sure! It never skips ahead or lags behind but keeps a steady rhythm to last the distance.

Despite all the praise it receives for great performance, **WISDOM** remains humble. It knows, many factors led up to its making. A major one is courage, the true backbone of **WISDOM**.

Courage is such a huge contributor that it would deserve a chapter of its own, but since we are limited to the 10 Essentials (in keeping with mountaineering rules), I would like to do it justice by bringing it to the limelight for a moment.

Courage brings pure exhilaration. The word alone is an adrenaline rush. It stares fear squarely in the face and says: "I am stronger than your threat! Where you say I *cannot*, I will show you that I *can*." Courage stands up for itself as well as for its companions. With courage, you have a strong warrior at your side who does not recognize hurdles. When God says: "Mountain move!" courage is right there and gets the job done. Courage knows *no* doubt. We certainly would have far fewer life experiences were it not for courage. It makes one dive into life bravely. **WISDOM** is very proud of it for good reasons.

Courage and **WISDOM** love to hold mutual admiration contests. Today, **WISDOM** gets in the last word and says: "Without you, I would not be who I AM." Courage falls silent for a second, obviously touched. However, it is not the type to linger on compliments and quickly turns to us weary hikers shouting enthusiastically: "Keep your chins up and trek along. You will arrive soon enough! And when you do, send us a postcard."

Here I stand, exhausted and dirty, ready to take a break to read the unexpected—note from heaven—which miraculously reached me in the middle of nowhere. I am one of those stragglers who could not keep up, but my companions have not forgotten me! Taking a deep breath, I look at the summit on the far horizon and at the trail sign in front of me → **Kingdom of Heaven - 8 hrs.** which at this point feels like an eternity ... but I cheer up as I decipher the handwritten scribbles of this magical postcard I am holding:

Take courage (says WISDOM)
you have not far to go !

I love you all...   God

PS: any other dream you thought you could not fulfill ?

Personal notes:

1) What is your understanding of the chapter? List three key elements.
2) What is your personal interpretation of **WISDOM**?
3) What aspects of **WISDOM** have you discovered within yourself?
4) What aspects of **WISDOM** would you like to cultivate or unearth?
5) What is your approach to making that happen?

....
....
....
....
....
....
....
....
....
....
....
....
....
....
....
....
....
....
....
....
....
....
....
....
....
....
....
....
....

Thank you for sharing your insights and inspiration!

Essential no. 7		FORGIVENESS

Where to purchase	:	a gift cannot be purchased; Christ was the original donor
Cost	:	$ 0.00—humility and willingness
Weight	:	0.00 lbs—errors weigh heavily; **FORGIVENESS** sheds weight
Where to pack	:	to be tucked close to LOVE and TRUTH, then wrapped in JOY

FORGIVENESS is a <u>bridge of light</u>, a <u>soldier of peace</u>, a <u>healer of wounds,</u> and the <u>remembrance of LOVE.</u>

These are just a few selected quotes of the ninety-nine ... flooding the horizon of a new dawn. Why is there so much to say about **FORGIVENESS**?

Our human imperfections depend on it daily.

Here on earth, we are learning to LOVE like a toddler is learning to walk. This is our predominant task and life lesson as humans. Where we stumble and fall, we need **FORGIVENESS** to give us the strength to get back up.

We are equally assured to be capable of *loving fully* one day, just as toddlers are assured to be *walking steadily* as they grow. We all take a toddler's success for granted. I encourage you to take *your* success to LOVE and live fully for granted as well.

You are <u>born and built to LOVE</u> like a toddler is <u>born and built to walk.</u>
LOVE is a matter of *willingness*, not a question of *capability*. You are *born* capable!

Once you *decide* to LOVE, you automatically know how to forgive since the ability to forgive stems from the capability to LOVE.

Is **FORGIVENESS** still an Essential then? Most definitely! It is our lifeline to heaven. I would consider it the most crucial after LOVE. As long as we are *not* proficient at loving yet, we depend on **FORGIVENESS** for survival.

God's **FORGIVENESS** is assured. Our guilt, pride, insecurities, and pains are the sentiments that hold us apart. Where **FORGIVENESS** needs to be practiced the most is among humans. We are less tolerant of one another than God is! To be forgiving is the only way to stop carrying hurt (or bitterness) into the future.

In order to start the **FORGIVENESS** process, we first need to acknowledge, we are all *worthy* to be forgiven because everybody is a child of God. He loves us, which is the basis of our worthiness. Then, we must humbly admit, we *all* have areas that need forgiving.

Forgiving oneself is as important as forgiving others and is often the only way to get started.
Once we know how to forgive ourselves, forgiving others becomes easier!

How *do* we forgive ourselves?

FORGIVENESS is easily granted from the viewpoint of LOVE.

Between needing and granting **FORGIVENESS** lies an abyss of judgment, resentment, hurt, and resistance. Christ *built* the bridge of **FORGIVENESS**—the only task we have is to *walk* across it—allowing our hearts to open again.

Let us count our blessings instead of holding on to painful memories that make our journey harder than necessary. We were not the *architects* of **FORGIVENESS**; we are the fortunate *beneficiarie*s!

Our only job is to *accept* the gift of **FORGIVENESS** and *grant* others the same privilege.

Can we make it to the Kingdom of Heaven without **FORGIVENESS**? The topic sounds a little *heavy*.

The answer is a definite NO. We all have to walk that bridge, but thankfully, we do not have to build it! **FORGIVENESS** only *seems* heavy until we let go of judgment. By itself it is very light.

OK, the Essential is getting packed! Let us get a head start on our practice. Our quotes at the beginning of the chapter are good reminders of how to make **FORGIVENESS** work:

   * **FORGIVENESS** is a bridge of light.
If caught in the dark, there is always some light peeking through the cracks. Follow that light ... it will surely lead you to heaven! If there is no *outer* light at all, there is always an *inner* light that can never be blotted out. Light leads to life. Turn toward it.

   * **FORGIVENESS** is a soldier of peace.
How can you be a soldier of peace? By forgiving yourself and others.

   * **FORGIVENESS** is a healer of wounds.
Wounds are the obvious side effect of a world that is *dis-connected* from God, which has the consequence of being *dis-connected* from LOVE. Where LOVE is missing, there are wounds to be healed. Only **FORGIVENESS** heals because it teaches you *not* to count how many times you have been *hurt* but to count how many people you have *healed* by forgiving.

   * **FORGIVENESS** is the remembrance of LOVE.
By remembering you *are* LOVE, you find the *willingness* to forgive. That is what LOVE does.

At last, some cautionary advice for the trails ahead. Beware, your *mind* can be stubborn at times and pretend **FORGIVENESS** is not within your reach. In those moments, I urge you to listen to your *heart*. It will remember exactly where you packed it!

Be assured, **FORGIVENESS** comes with a huge reward:

gladness of the heart.

AMEN

Personal notes:

1) What is your understanding of the chapter? List three key elements.
2) What is your personal interpretation of **FORGIVENESS**?
3) What aspects of **FORGIVENESS** have you discovered within yourself?
4) What aspects of **FORGIVENESS** would you like to cultivate or unearth?
5) What is your approach to making that happen?

Thank you for sharing your insights and inspiration!

Essential no. 8   HUMOR

Where to purchase	:	deep in your belly
Cost	:	$ 0.00—trade in seriousness for **HUMOR**
Weight	:	0.00 lbs—with **HUMOR**, heaviness drops off fast
Where to pack	:	next to JOY

Why pack **HUMOR**?

You are kidding, right? Of course, I am kidding! We are discussing **HUMOR**, after all.

Before we get too wrapped up in weighing the odds, let me tell you, **HUMOR** not only packs itself, but it magically does away with unwanted bulk.

It is lighthearted in the face of *seriousness* and effectively alleviates *worry*—two heavy items we would rather *not* pack. That is exactly why we are bringing **HUMOR**. It is very savvy at ditching weight, which is a backpacker's favorite downtime occupation!

HUMOR slices stuffiness with the precision of a Samurai. Like a sword, it cuts a rip through the fog, and all stuffiness is gone. It lifts any kind of oppression, transforms sorrow, and does not fret. **HUMOR** introduces a moment of heaven where all negatives are suspended. It knows how to make people smile. At times it gets them laughing so hard that they literally cry, which shakes all tension loose (a great benefit when trekking)!

What **HUMOR** does best (and it does it without trying): It shifts our focus from *terrible to acceptable* and from *unbearable to bearable*, always seeing the bright side of life! Our 8th Essential is definitely an optimist and more often than not the life of the party. It has the unique skill to put *doom and gloom* in reverse.

Naturally, everyone is fond of **HUMOR**. What more can one ask of an Essential?

Now is the perfect moment to present you with a humorous riddle :)

What do you do when you come to a fork in the trail?

Pick it up and go!

(… use the fork for the next "fancy meal" in the woods … ha,ha,ha)

See how easy and spontaneous decision-making can be?

HUMOR gives the gift of JOY, creating an atmosphere of lightness. People are grateful for the lightheartedness offered and reward HUMOR by being supportive. Hence, things fall into place with *ease*.

JOY, our 2nd Essential, adores HUMOR. They have become fast buddies ever since they laid eyes on each other. HUMOR nourishes JOY in a way that nobody else can.

When they play, which is often, HUMOR tends to be the instigator of the two and the first to crack a joke. JOY, on the other hand, is HUMOR's best audience and never misses a beat expressing spontaneous delight! Needless to say, they make a fabulous pair. Just being around them lightens everyone's mood. If you ever wonder whether you have lost your path, simply follow their laughter (which is a good alternative if you have not learned the art of navigation yet)!

But there is more to their silliness than meets the eye. They are both *tactfully* uplifting.

In our careful selection of Essentials, we asked them all to make a pledge: to never use their skills in bad taste. HUMOR had to agree not to make jokes that are degrading, and JOY had to promise not to laugh *at* people but laugh *with* people. I must say, so far, they have been very ethical in that regard. All Essentials are called to their highest standard, not to fall short of entering the Kingdom of Heaven.

Since we are practicing for the long haul, let me ask you an important question. When have you last had a really great belly laugh? Do you recall how contagious it was? Laughing *with* someone can have such a ripple effect, you may end up laughing for hours! I have a fond memory of cruising on a tour boat in the harbor of San Diego when "suddenly" we started laughing so hard and simply could *not* stop! We tried, but pretty soon we were rolling in tears, holding on to our bellies for dear life. What a day on the water ...

If you have not laughed in a while, it is time to walk to the next mirror in sight. Start with a smile and expand from there. Grimacing might help. If you still cannot laugh, you may possibly suffer the serious condition of taking yourself far too seriously! Try again until you are having a jolly good laugh with yourself. You cannot possibly fail at this exercise. You have to admit—your funny faces look hilarious in the mirror :)

Laughing is a cure to invite often. HUMOR is a most entertaining guest and an affordable doctor on top. It spares us all kinds of headaches and the cost of an EMT (Emergency Medical Technician).

As to whether it is a worthy Essential to bring? It looks like we have a unanimous vote!

When things get tough, rely on HUMOR. You can count on it in the oddest of moments. The very instant I say this, I hear HUMOR giggle in the background:

"See you in the Kingdom of Heaven—it would be laughable not to reach it."

HUMOR makes me smile one more time as I watch my last lingering doubts ... vanishing into thin air!

AMEN

Personal notes:

1) What is your understanding of the chapter? List three key elements.
2) What is your personal interpretation of **HUMOR**?
3) What aspects of **HUMOR** have you discovered within yourself?
4) What aspects of **HUMOR** would you like to cultivate or unearth?
5) What is your approach to making that happen?

Thank you for sharing your insights and inspiration!

Essential no. 9		ART

Where to purchase	:	in your soul
Cost	:	$ 0.00—imagination and a sense of beauty
Weight	:	0.00 lbs—**ART** walks lightly and with grace
Where to pack	:	in the neighborhood of LOVE and JOY

Thou ART beautiful.

You are a living sculpture: *moving, thinking, feeling, experiencing,* and *expressing.* You have a breath and a heartbeat—are warm to the touch—and one of a kind. Light is shining from *within* you. No spotlight is needed. You are naturally brilliant!

Find a mirror and look into your eyes for a moment. Do not judge your looks today. Go beyond the surface and quietly *meet* yourself. What are you seeing?

Life itself is looking straight at you!

Simply amazing. God indeed is the ultimate artist, and YOU are His masterpiece.

Each one of us is born a *unique* masterpiece whom God eternally treasures.

How does He express this on a daily basis? With His unending LOVE. No matter what we do, no matter how we look, He loves us (even on a bad hair day)!

You might still wrestle with the fact of being a *masterpiece*? The TRUTH is you *are*. At birth, God passed on a gene called LOVE which is the secret ingredient of a masterpiece.

OK, I rest my case, but why on earth bring **ART** on a backpacking trip? Does this not seem utterly impractical? So far, we have been bare minimalists, and now we are suddenly hauling **ART** up the hill?

As much as **ART** appears to be a luxury item, it actually has the characteristics of a survival tool (... a survival tool for the soul, to be precise) which qualifies it as an Essential.

ART has a knack for seeing beauty along the way, which nourishes your soul and makes you momentarily forget the effort involved. An animated soul has perseverance and stamina. **ART** puts a song in your heart and a bounce in your step, and before you know it, you have gone the extra mile. Somehow, you always feel encouraged in its company because it sees you for who you *truly* are.

Where rough terrain and heavy packs have a tendency to weigh you down, **ART** is lifting you up!

With its power of inspiration, it defies gravity in a sense. **ART** makes you smile and marvel at things, taking your focus off of hardship.

Graceful movement is a JOY to watch and a pure melody in motion. Precise, deliberate steps are proven to be less accident-prone. **ART** helps you tread lightly, preserving precious energy!

By now, we have collected enough evidence to be convinced of **ART**'s usefulness and contribution to safety, but how are we going to pack it?

ART is generally viewed as an *object*, something outside of us, but in reality it is not. *Artful living* has very little to do with an object. YOU are **ART** in motion!

To be *fully alive* and *completely yourself* ... is the greatest **ART** of all.

Nothing strengthens the immune system more than genuine self-expression! **ART** wisely celebrates the uniqueness and recognizes each person as an irreplaceable part of the grand puzzle. Together, we make the most perfect **ART** piece called humankind, particularly beautiful when *kind*.

Realizing we are **ART** form—in body, mind, and soul—magically resolves the whole dilemma of weight and space. By simply showing up and deciding to be part of this adventure, we are bringing **ART** *naturally* with us. No more concerns whether it might be too heavy or too bulky, we are it!

Oddly enough, all of our Essentials (as important as they are) do not weigh a single ounce. No purchases need to be made, nor are there any price tags to worry about, and our packs remain ultra-light.
What a delight :)

I can hardly wait to be part of our *walking* **ART** gallery! How about you?

A = Are you?

R = Ready?

T = To be yourself?

That is all it takes. Come and grace the trails with your *presence.*

Your footprints will leave a legacy behind and a sense of direction for others to follow, leading us straight to the Kingdom of Heaven! What better direction could you possibly instill?

Thou ART beautiful.

Thank you for *accepting* your heritage.

AMEN

Personal notes:

1) What is your understanding of the chapter? List three key elements.
2) What is your personal interpretation of **ART**?
3) What aspects of **ART** have you discovered within yourself?
4) What aspects of **ART** would you like to cultivate or unearth?
5) What is your approach to making that happen?

Thank you for sharing your insights and inspiration!

Essential no. 10		SIMPLICITY

Where to purchase	:	in your heart
Cost	:	$ 0.00—and detachment
Weight	:	0.00 lbs—**SIMPLICITY** packs light
Where to pack	:	LOVE and God share their space with **SIMPLICITY**

SIMPLICITY is our 10th and final Essential—a true hero—because it knows how to *simplify complexity*. With its keen eye for essence, it handpicked the other nine Essentials, ensuring we make it through the eye of the needle to the Kingdom of Heaven! It bravely stripped us from the unnecessary bulk without jeopardizing our safety, quality, or goal.

God Himself marvels at the wise choices **SIMPLICITY** made and says: "You know, my child, by bringing LOVE, JOY, TRUTH, FREEDOM, RESPONSIBILITY, WISDOM, FORGIVENESS, HUMOR, ART, and **SIMPLICITY** on this trip, you really do not need *me* to come along—as I AM in all these things—and most of all in YOU."

"I AM **SIMPLICITY** in person."

"While the rest of the world is busy searching for me in the complexity of life, I AM residing in YOU, in the stillness of your heart. You, my child, have found me! Congratulations, dear." **SIMPLICITY** is awestruck, momentarily blushes, and asks: "Tell me, God, where are we going from here? We have prepared for so long to reach the Kingdom of Heaven."

"Well, my child, you have arrived!"

"It took all this time for your mind to realize that the seemingly longest and steepest journey is in reality the shortest and simplest of all. *Going within* does not cost you a dime, is hardly a distance to speak of, takes no time nor effort, and is certainly not a matter of weight."

"The Kingdom of Heaven … God … as well as **SIMPLICITY** are all to be found in your wonderful heart! You have never been apart from me. Separation is a construct of a fearful mind but actually an impossibility."

Perplexed at the TRUTH of it all, **SIMPLICITY** sighs with audible relief:

"WHO WOULD HAVE EVER THOUGHT IT IS THAT … SIMPLE …!"

God observes my puzzled mind and adds with a soft whisper: "It is called self-acceptance, dear."

Welcome HOME.
Let the celebration begin.

AMEN

Personal notes:

1) What is your understanding of the chapter? List three key elements.
2) What is your personal interpretation of **SIMPLICITY**?
3) What aspects of **SIMPLICITY** have you discovered within yourself?
4) What aspects of **SIMPLICITY** would you like to cultivate or unearth?
5) What is your approach to making that happen?

....
....
....
....
....
....
....
....
....
....
....
....
....
....
....
....
....
....
....
....
....
....
....
....
....
....
....

Thank you for sharing your insights and inspiration!

EPILOGUE

A quick re-cap and reference guide to important life principles:

- The greatest values in life we all yearn for are not *things* we can buy with money. They are *qualities* found inside our hearts. We *are* what most of us spend a whole lifetime *looking* for! **LOVE** and **JOY** are our very nature.

- On our deathbed, we do not think about a car, a bank account, or owning a boat. We think about **LOVE** and **JOY**. Have we *loved* enough? Have we been *loved*? Have we had and *shared* **JOY**? Let your imaginary deathbed be your teacher of how to live a life of no regrets.

- **LOVE** is a *magnet*. It attracts all the things we need. God, our Father, sustains us through **LOVE**. He created us as *magnets* of **LOVE** to never be wanting. Our job is to be *fearless*. Being **LOVE** gives us the courage not to fear. FEAR is **F**alse **E**vidence **A**ppearing **R**eal. It is a self-made infliction, forgetting we *are* **LOVE**. Fear repels and pushes away what we desire the most. Know thyself as **LOVE**, and the things of your dreams come to you!

- This book invites you to *become* the Essentials. In truth, you *are* them already. Your work consists of peeling away the lies that tell you otherwise. Underneath, you are your authentic, brilliant self. Ask your heart to reveal itself. It is your *inner* heaven.

Now that we have established, we have nowhere to go except *within* ...
what happens with our backpacking trip?

Take yourself for a pleasure loop in the woods! There is no important destination to reach.
Getting ready for this trip made you *meet* yourself. YOU are the destination!

Where you go and what you do in life is completely up to you.
It is your free will choice, a gift of self-determination, offered to you by God.
He honors you deeply. That is why He gave you FREEDOM.

Do what you **LOVE** the most, and you will be positively infectious!
Spread your ease (instead of *dis*-ease). Ease is a reality of **LOVE**.

Demonstrate a life of Heaven on Earth. You will please God more than you can fathom.

HEAVEN is where you **LOVE**.

You do not have to *die* to experience heaven. It wants to occupy all of earth.
YOU are the one who can make that happen!

How?
Invite **LOVE**, be **LOVE**, express **LOVE**.
Breathe it in ... and ... breathe it out.

SIGN-UP SHEET

I recognize, **I AM** a child of God and therefore **LOVE**.
KINDNESS is what I am here to share.

I am ready to claim my inheritance—**LOVE**—and willing to help others claim their own.
JOY is our new shared wealth!

AMEN

Your Signature: .... Date: ....

Trail-notes and personal impressions. Write down your greatest discoveries and realizations:

....
....
....
....
....
....
....
....
....
....
....
....
....
....
....

Your personal **Practice Book** is attached to *internalize* each Essential on an intimate basis.
Go on a *daily adventure*—experience *daily success*!

Part II   The **Practice Book** of
GOD in a backpack

Your personal

Practice Book

Practice	Essential no. 1	LOVE
Practice	Essential no. 2	JOY
Practice	Essential no. 3	TRUTH
Practice	Essential no. 4	FREEDOM
Practice	Essential no. 5	RESPONSIBILITY
Practice	Essential no. 6	WISDOM
Practice	Essential no. 7	FORGIVENESS
Practice	Essential no. 8	HUMOR
Practice	Essential no. 9	ART
Practice	Essential no. 10	SIMPLICITY

Spiritual backpacking

Now comes the time we go *within* to deepen each theme, to *become* it, to *personify* it
with every fiber of our being!

This is where the rubber meets the road
... except in our case ...
it is the rubber of our trail shoes touching the soft ground of Mother Earth.
What a refreshing difference!

We are gently stepping into our truth, with hearts wide open, embracing the light.
Enlivened by the beauty of our horizon and refreshed by a gentle breeze.
Striding step by step * awake and conscious * toward our birthright,

the Kingdom of Heaven

... wandering ...
on wooded *quiet* trails within
where our *souls* rest gently,
joyously awaiting our arrival home.

We step into our **LOVE** we are born to be!

We step into our **JOY** we are born to be!

We step into our **TRUTH** we are born to be!

We step into our **FREEDOM** we are born to be!

We step into our **RESPONSIBILITY** we are born to be!

We step into our **WISDOM** we are born to be!

We step into our **FORGIVENESS** we are born to be!

We step into our **HUMOR** we are born to be!

We step into our **ART** we are born to be!

We step into our **SIMPLICITY** we are born to be!

Enjoying the peace our journey brings * an inner peace * we are now able to share with others.

Today we become experts at **LOVE.** Here is how to:

Receive it—**Be** it—**Share** it.

This is our slogan and golden thread throughout the entire Practice Book
to *deeply internalize* the 10 Essentials and to make them stick to our soul.

By launching into life with one exercise page a day, we are becoming *a living embodiment* of each Essential,
grooming ourselves to be successful and kindhearted **HEAVEN**on**EARTH** citizens.

Inspired by the heart, we are creating a world where everybody has a place of safety and happiness to enjoy.
A vibrant human society—sharing resources and responsibilities fairly—as God intended.

This section of our instruction manual to heaven serves the purpose of *practically applying*
what we have learned in the prepping portion of **GOD in a backpack.**

Without further ado, let us get started with our valuable practice called * The BEST ME that I CAN BE *
Bliss is homegrown. No fertilizer necessary, just a little LOVE.

Dive into these exercises with glee—knowing YOU are going HOME—with each step of conviction.
Your soul has been waiting for your arrival for (what seems like) an eternity!

This is—where and how—YOU start:

Each morning, assume the position of the **HEAVEN**on**EARTH** symbol, the letter **Y.**

Your body, mind, and soul are becoming a receptive **Y.** Stretch your arms high. Reach for the sky!

The letter **Y** is the first letter of the word **YES**. It is also the first letter of the word **YOU**.

Start each day by saying:

1) **Y**ES => to the goodness of heaven, pouring all its riches into **Y**OU as **Y**OU open up.
2) **Y**ES => to **Y**OUR Self, acknowledging **Y**OUR own goodness and accepting **Y**OUR worthiness.

This is how **Y**OU receive **blessings** from heaven every day,
serving **Y**OU
to personally **thrive** and generously **share** with others.

Heaven on Earth©

This is what today's **LOVE** exercise looks like for YOU personally:

Start by re-reading the LOVE chapter (Essential no. 1) in **GOD in a backpack** to get inspired.
Then do the following exercises:

1) **Receive** love from heaven by becoming the letter **Y** with your body. Open up and feel love *pour* into you. This is "your fuel station" moment: Fuel up on all the love you think you need for the day. Your fuel tank is your heart, to fill at your convenience. Heaven never runs out of fuel; it is your free gas station for life. No money is required—everybody has equal access—and it is conveniently located. Your maximum driving distance is the distance between your hand and your heart. Reach for your heart right now, and feel your own heartbeat. It is beating for *you* because it *loves* you. Imagine heaven (your gas station) connected via a hose with your heart (your gas tank). The gas you are pumping is love! Store plenty of it daily. Love from above is your *vertical* gift from heaven without a price tag, running your engine called life.

The letter **Y** is a symbol of *openness,* making **HEAVEN**on**EARTH** available to you as a *tangible* reality. Stretch into it with a wide-open heart and without the slightest restraint. Receive! There is no cap on heaven's bounty. You are a child of God and worthy of it all. Make heaven happy by saying YES. It wants nothing more than to nourish you, so you shall never thirst or hunger for love again. Over time, while practicing your daily **Y**, anxieties and doubts will vanish. You will experience repeatedly how much heaven loves you, no matter your behavior or how your day went.
Heaven and God are incapable of denying you love. Accept the gift!
Write on your next page how you felt love pour into you today. Include experiences of receiving love *horizontally* (from humans, animals, nature, life, and yourself!). Enjoy re-visiting today's events while pondering God and your divine connection with the origin of life.

Feel into your eternal relationship with the creator, which can never be severed. Savor this beautiful feeling of reassurance, to be loved always, without exception!

2) **Be** love. Start your day by being loving—toward your own self. You deserve your loving attention. Enjoy this precious moment! This is your love affair with self and quite heartwarming. You will never forget personal experiences—they are truly memorable and embedded forever in your being. Thank yourself for taking the time to love your being today. Your notes will reflect deep gratitude and joy.

3) **Share** love. Randomly pick somebody or something to love today, in a planned or spontaneous way. In a moment when life offers you the opportunity. Describe in specific details how you chose to share your love, how it felt to the person you loved, and how it affected you. You will find empty pages happily waiting for your journal entry. Bathe yourself in the aftermath of love. Observe your inner and outer smile :)

It truly feels good ... to love.

Your in-depth journal notes:

1) **Receive** LOVE

Mention three specific experiences in your practice of receiving LOVE today.

How did you receive LOVE? What did you do? How did you feel?

I received LOVE *vertically* (from heaven) by… :

....
....
....
....
....
....
....
....
....
....
....
....
....

I received LOVE *horizontally* (from people, animals, nature, life circumstances) by… :

....
....
....
....
....
....
....
....
....
....
....
....
....

Bravo—well done!

Your in-depth journal notes:

2) **Be** LOVE

Mention three specific experiences in your practice of being LOVE today.

What made you realize you *are* LOVE? What did you do and experience? How did you feel?

....
....
....
....
....
....
....
....
....
....
....
....
....
....
....
....
....
....
....
....
....
....
....
....
....
....
....
....
....
....

Fantastic—good job!

Your in-depth journal notes:

3) **Share** LOVE

Mention three specific experiences in your practice of sharing LOVE today.

How did you share LOVE with others? How did your LOVE affect them? How did you feel?

....
....
....
....
....
....
....
....
....
....
....
....
....
....
....
....
....
....
....
....
....
....
....
....
....
....
....
....
....
....
....
....

Excellent! YOU are on a brave journey. I am truly proud of YOU.

Today we become experts at **JOY.** Here is how to:

Receive it—**Be** it—**Share** it.

Re-read this whole page. There are small differences for you to discover. It is mostly a repetition *on purpose*. This is how we best learn! We *linger* on truthful facts of life, and we *focus* on who we want to be.

* **Receive** it—**Be** it—**Share** it * is our slogan and golden thread throughout the entire Practice Book to *deeply internalize* the <u>10 Essentials</u> and to make them stick to our soul.

By launching into life with one exercise page a day, we are becoming *a living embodiment* of each Essential, grooming ourselves to be successful and kindhearted **HEAVEN**on**EARTH** citizens.

Inspired by the heart, we are creating a world where everybody has a place of safety and happiness to enjoy. A vibrant human society—sharing resources and responsibilities fairly—as God intended.

This section of our instruction manual to heaven serves the purpose of *practically applying* what we have learned in the prepping portion of **GOD in a backpack.**

Without further ado, let us get started with our valuable practice called * The BEST ME that I CAN BE * Bliss is homegrown. No fertilizer necessary, just a little JOY.

Dive into these exercises with glee—knowing YOU are going HOME—with each step of conviction. Your soul has been waiting for your arrival for (what seems like) an eternity!

<u>This is—where and how—YOU start</u>:

Each morning, assume the position of the **HEAVEN**on**EARTH** symbol, the letter **Y.**

Your body, mind, and soul are becoming a receptive **Y.** Stretch your arms high. Reach for the sky!

The letter **Y** is the first letter of the word **Y**ES. It is also the first letter of the word **Y**OU.

<u>Start each day by saying</u>:

1) **Y**ES => to the goodness of heaven, pouring all its riches into **Y**OU as **Y**OU open up.
2) **Y**ES => to **Y**OUR Self, acknowledging **Y**OUR own goodness and accepting **Y**OUR worthiness.

This is how **Y**OU receive **blessings** from heaven every day,
serving **Y**OU
to personally **thrive** and generously **share** with others.

Heaven on Earth©

This is what today's **JOY** exercise looks like for YOU personally:

Start by re-reading the JOY chapter (Essential no. 2) in **GOD in a backpack** to get inspired.
Then do the following exercises:

1) **Receive** joy from heaven, from people, from yourself, from nature, or any other circumstance that joyfully presents itself today. Be attentive and collect your jewels! Life is truly magical. Have you stopped to look and see? Beauty and magic show up when you observe. Focus on the wonder of your breath for a minute. Feel it course through your nostrils and into your body. What a momentous gift of life! You are never forgotten. God keeps you alive with every breath you take whether you think about it or not and without lifting a finger. Do you realize the *fortune* you are born with and the *ease* you have been granted? You must be bubbling over with joy! Take notes with a song in your heart, thankfully reflecting how effortlessly joy came your way today.

2) **Be** joy. Being joyous is most contagious and the best influence in the world. If you want to change the world, be joyous! Joy has a natural stage presence. It *shines* brilliantly and *draws* attention wherever it goes. Its radiance and magnetism are of equal strength. Joy is a spotlight unto itself. Nobody can overlook it because it emits so much light! Therein lies its irresistible power. This day is dedicated to refreshing your memory of how to live your life with joy: <u>As you **love**, so will be the measure of your **joy**</u>! You now *own* the world's most sought-after recipe of how to be happy. Become the example, so others may also experience that **joy** is right around the corner from **love**. Journal on how you found inner joy today. What brought it about?

I can see your glow from afar!

3) **Share** joy. Look forward to sharing joy with the world. Today, tomorrow, and every day! It is time to be joyous together. There is nothing to hold back and everything to give freely. You are abundantly blessed. All the goodness and joy you are experiencing this day will be replenished again tomorrow. You *receive* enough for the day, *empty* yourself for others during the day, give *thanks* in the evening for all that you have received and were able to give, and the cycle repeats itself as you **open** your arms wide again the next day! Through personal experience you have discovered the source of love to *flow* continuously. It is a forever well-spring you can tap into at any moment of your day. Life is an eternal river, bringing joy to the riverbank where you pause for picnics. A river has its *source* high up in the mountains where a small pond -> feeds a tiny creek -> becomes a stream -> then a river. Likewise, all goodness flows from *above* (heaven) and reaches you *within* (heart). The connection between the two (heaven -> heart) is the invisible silver cord, your lifeline and love current pulsating between God and you. This stream of love from heaven is feeding your heart. The result is pure joy!

When you share joy with others, your heart pulsates and dances with theirs. Write about today's experiences of sharing joy with people. Describe how their eyes were glistening and how their spark of life was clearly visible. Tell us where your joy came from and why you have such *trust* that you will never run out. I look forward to your journal entry and can feel your smile in the atmosphere ... it is very palpable!

No feeling is ever felt alone—we are all connected—thank God.

Your in-depth journal notes:

1) **Receive** JOY

Mention three specific experiences in your practice of receiving JOY today.

How did you receive JOY? What did you do? How did you feel?

I received JOY *vertically* (from heaven) by... :

....
....
....
....
....
....
....
....
....
....
....
....
....
....

I received JOY *horizontally* (from people, animals, nature, life circumstances) by... :

....
....
....
....
....
....
....
....
....
....
....
....
....

Bravo—well done!

Your in-depth journal notes:

2) **Be** JOY

Mention three specific experiences in your practice of being JOY today.

How were you joyous with your own self? What did you do and experience?

....
....
....
....
....
....
....
....
....
....
....
....
....
....
....
....
....
....
....
....
....
....
....
....
....
....
....
....

Fantastic—good job!

Your in-depth journal notes:

3) **Share** JOY

Mention three specific experiences in your practice of sharing JOY today.

How did you share JOY with others? Whom did you share it with? How did that affect them (and you)?

....

....

....

....

....

....

....

....

....

....

....

....

....

....

....

....

....

....

....

....

....

....

....

....

....

....

....

....

....

....

Excellent! YOU are on a brave journey. I am truly proud of YOU.

Today we become experts at **TRUTH.** Here is how to:

Receive it—Be it—Share it.

Re-read this whole page. There are small differences for you to discover. It is mostly a repetition *on purpose.* This is how we best learn! We *linger* on truthful facts of life, and we *focus* on who we want to be.

* Receive it—**Be** it—**Share** it * is our slogan and golden thread throughout the entire Practice Book to *deeply internalize* the 10 Essentials and to make them stick to our soul.

By launching into life with one exercise page a day, we are becoming *a living embodiment* of each Essential, grooming ourselves to be successful and kindhearted **HEAVEN**on**EARTH** citizens.

Inspired by the heart, we are creating a world where everybody has a place of safety and happiness to enjoy. A vibrant human society—sharing resources and responsibilities fairly—as God intended.

This section of our instruction manual to heaven serves the purpose of *practically applying* what we have learned in the prepping portion of **GOD in a backpack.**

Without further ado, let us get started with our valuable practice called * The BEST ME that I CAN BE * Bliss is homegrown. No fertilizer necessary, just a little TRUTH.

Dive into these exercises with glee—knowing YOU are going HOME—with each step of conviction. Your soul has been waiting for your arrival for (what seems like) an eternity!

This is—where and how—YOU start:

Each morning, assume the position of the **HEAVEN**on**EARTH** symbol, the letter **Y.**

Your body, mind, and soul are becoming a receptive **Y.** Stretch your arms high. Reach for the sky!

The letter **Y** is the first letter of the word **Y**ES. It is also the first letter of the word **Y**OU.

Start each day by saying:

1) **Y**ES => to the goodness of heaven, pouring all its riches into **Y**OU as **Y**OU open up.
2) **Y**ES => to **Y**OUR Self, acknowledging **Y**OUR own goodness and accepting **Y**OUR worthiness.

This is how **Y**OU receive **blessings** from heaven every day,
serving **Y**OU
to personally **thrive** and generously **share** with others.

Heaven on Earth©

This is what today's **TRUTH** exercise looks like for YOU personally:

Start by re-reading the TRUTH chapter (Essential no. 3) in **GOD in a backpack** to get inspired.
Then do the following exercises:

1) **Receive** truth. Whenever, wherever, however you can. It is a very important commodity for clarity in life. Without it, we do not know what is up or what is down, what is right or what is wrong. Amid confusion, we cannot think, feel, or see clearly. We need to defog the window of our inner and outer vision. The work is called unclogging the filter or unplugging the drain. Truth is a good and thorough flush in our lives. It unblocks stagnation, chases darkness and vagueness away, clears confusion and uncertainty, and, of course, takes care of lies. It makes one see the lay of the land, so to speak, to realize what needs fixing. Without truth, we do not know where to start with the clean-up and how to go about it. Truth disentangles messiness, lifts heaviness, and sets tension and constriction *free*. With truth, we can start anew! Receive truth from heaven, from people, and life itself. What might feel uncomfortable at first is really a blessing in disguise. Feeling uncomfortable should not steer you away from receiving truth. Invite it at all costs—it is medicine for the soul. Write in your journal how *receiving* truth has helped you resolve things today. Be brave, be glad. You will feel a ton lighter!

2) **Be** truth. When you live life from transparency rather than hiding, nothing gets in the way of experiencing joy. You do not have to dodge any bullets or be in fear of being found out. By choosing to be truthful, you live a life of no secrets, have no taboos, and are not ashamed of anything. You will reach a point in your life where you are only comfortable living most *truthfully* because it is the easiest, most worry-free way to live. Hiding takes effort. Truth provides deep comfort and relaxation. God created us with all the necessary ingredients to live a good life. The main ingredient is love, which *contains* truth. We can ask love to help us *recover* truth. It will lend us the courage to shed lies and set our conscience free! Conscience is our inner meter that knows how much of our truth is buried. It presses against our soul, nudging us to come clean. Open up to your inner truth and journal about your peeling process—it feels like shedding pounds. Today is your "beauty spa" of the soul.
Enjoy the cleanse!

3) **Share** truth. Share yourself truthfully with others, as God shares Himself with you. He will never lie to you, nor shall you lie to others. Tell people how beautiful they are. Share with them "the good news" about the kind of life they can *choose* to live. Invite them on your backpacking trip so that the fun of good living may go round-and-round for all to enjoy! We are family and family *shares*. Your journaling will feel very light. To celebrate your progress today, truth dropped off a personal gift at your doorstep:

Your in-depth journal notes:

1) **Receive** TRUTH

Mention three specific experiences in your practice of receiving TRUTH today.

How did you receive TRUTH? How did that affect you?

I received TRUTH *vertically* (from heaven) by… :

....
....
....
....
....
....
....
....
....
....
....
....
....
....

I received TRUTH *horizontally* (from people, animals, nature, life circumstances) by… :

....
....
....
....
....
....
....
....
....
....
....
....
....
....

Bravo—well done!

Your in-depth journal notes:

2) **Be** TRUTH

Mention three specific experiences in your practice of being TRUTH today.

How were you truthful with yourself? What did you do? How did you feel?

....

....

....

....

....

....

....

....

....

....

....

....

....

....

....

....

....

....

....

....

....

....

....

....

....

....

....

....

Fantastic—good job!

Your in-depth journal notes:

3) **Share** TRUTH

Mention three specific experiences in your practice of sharing TRUTH today.

How did you share TRUTH with others? How did that affect them (and you)?

....
....
....
....
....
....
....
....
....
....
....
....
....
....
....
....
....
....
....
....
....
....
....
....
....
....
....
....
....
....

Excellent! YOU are on a brave journey. I am truly proud of YOU.

Today we become experts at **FREEDOM.** Here is how to:

Receive it—**Be** it—**Share** it.

Re-read this whole page. There are small differences for you to discover. It is mostly a repetition *on purpose.* This is how we best learn! We *linger* on truthful facts of life, and we *focus* on who we want to be.

* Receive it—**Be** it—**Share** it * is our slogan and golden thread throughout the entire Practice Book to *deeply internalize* the 10 Essentials and to make them stick to our soul.

By launching into life with one exercise page a day, we are becoming *a living embodiment* of each Essential, grooming ourselves to be successful and kindhearted **HEAVEN**on**EARTH** citizens.

Inspired by the heart, we are creating a world where everybody has a place of safety and happiness to enjoy. A vibrant human society—sharing resources and responsibilities fairly—as God intended.

This section of our instruction manual to heaven serves the purpose of *practically applying* what we have learned in the prepping portion of **GOD in a backpack.**

Without further ado, let us get started with our valuable practice called * The BEST ME that I CAN BE * Bliss is homegrown. No fertilizer necessary, just a little FREEDOM.

Dive into these exercises with glee—knowing YOU are going HOME—with each step of conviction. Your soul has been waiting for your arrival for (what seems like) an eternity!

This is—where and how—YOU start:

Each morning, assume the position of the **HEAVEN**on**EARTH** symbol, the letter **Y.**

Your body, mind, and soul are becoming a receptive **Y.** Stretch your arms high. Reach for the sky!

The letter **Y** is the first letter of the word **YES**. It is also the first letter of the word **YOU**.

Start each day by saying:

1) **Y**ES => to the goodness of heaven, pouring all its riches into **YOU** as **YOU** open up.
2) **Y**ES => to **Y**OUR Self, acknowledging **Y**OUR own goodness and accepting **Y**OUR worthiness.

This is how **YOU** receive **blessings** from heaven every day,
serving **YOU**
to personally **thrive** and generously **share** with others.

Heaven on Earth©

This is what today's **FREEDOM** exercise looks like for YOU personally:

Start by re-reading the FREEDOM chapter (Essential no. 4) in **GOD in a backpack** to get inspired.
Then do the following exercises:

1) **Receive** freedom from *within*. That is your place of true authority. God placed it there. His and your authority are shared, forever intertwined and inseparable. He and you are ONE. Can you imagine God *not* being free? You are His child and equally free because He made you in His image. Do not ask others for permission to be free—this is *your* personal freedom and birthright. God knows of no other existence than freedom. He set us all *free* because He loves and trusts us without question. Bondage is not the way of love. Freedom is! You are love, and in its hands, freedom is safe. Write in your journal how *receiving* freedom prompted you to live to the fullest today.

2) **Be** freedom. Being free is your nature and rightful experience. Freedom is yours to be lived and enjoyed and starts *within*. Where else would it be felt and experienced on a personal level? Allow yourself freedom! It is one of the many natural treasures God generously passed on when He gave you life. *Free* is how He created you to be. Live it, be it, breathe it, savor it. When you love yourself truly, you never abuse freedom but treat it as precious. Guard freedom with your life, yet unafraid, launch yourself courageously into the unknown. Express in your journal how good it feels to be free.

Write as you feel the air of adventure blow through your hair!

3) **Share** freedom. Here is where mutuality comes in. What does that mean? We cannot really "give or allow" another person freedom since freedom is a gift from God, a privilege that has already been granted. What we are here on earth to learn is to **accept** our birthright of being free while **honoring** the freedom of each person, including our own. Honoring freedom means we live it *responsibly* as not to lose the privilege.

Take flight and enjoy the sight ...

I look forward to your tales of freedom—surely, they will be inspiring! Share with your journal where your adventures took you. And next time, bring me with you, will you?

I can hardly wait.

Your in-depth journal notes:

1) **Receive** FREEDOM

Mention three specific experiences in your practice of receiving FREEDOM today.

How did you receive FREEDOM? What did you do? What feelings did your actions provoke?

I received FREEDOM *vertically* (from heaven) by... :

....
....
....
....
....
....
....
....
....
....
....
....
....
....

I received FREEDOM *horizontally* (from people, animals, nature, life circumstances) by... :

....
....
....
....
....
....
....
....
....
....
....
....
....
....

Bravo—well done!

Your in-depth journal notes:

2) **Be** FREEDOM

Mention three specific experiences in your practice of being FREEDOM today.

How were you freeing yourself? How did that make you feel?

....

....

....

....

....

....

....

....

....

....

....

....

....

....

....

....

....

....

....

....

....

....

....

....

....

....

....

Fantastic—good job!

Your in-depth journal notes:

3) **Share** FREEDOM

Mention three specific experiences in your practice of sharing FREEDOM today.

How did you share FREEDOM with others? How did that make them (and you) feel?

....
....
....
....
....
....
....
....
....
....
....
....
....
....
....
....
....
....
....
....
....
....
....
....
....
....
....
....
....
....
....

Excellent! YOU are on a brave journey. I am truly proud of YOU.

Today we become experts at **RESPONSIBILITY.** Here is how to:

Receive it—**Be** it—**Share** it.

Re-read this whole page. There are small differences for you to discover. It is mostly a repetition *on purpose*. This is how we best learn! We *linger* on truthful facts of life, and we *focus* on who we want to be.

* **Receive** it—**Be** it—**Share** it * is our slogan and golden thread throughout the entire Practice Book to *deeply internalize* the 10 Essentials and to make them stick to our soul.

By launching into life with one exercise page a day, we are becoming *a living embodiment* of each Essential, grooming ourselves to be successful and kindhearted **HEAVEN**on**EARTH** citizens.

Inspired by the heart, we are creating a world where everybody has a place of safety and happiness to enjoy. A vibrant human society—sharing resources and responsibilities fairly—as God intended.

This section of our instruction manual to heaven serves the purpose of *practically applying* what we have learned in the prepping portion of **GOD in a backpack.**

Without further ado, let us get started with our valuable practice called * The BEST ME that I CAN BE * Bliss is homegrown. No fertilizer necessary, just a little RESPONSIBILITY.

Dive into these exercises with glee—knowing YOU are going HOME—with each step of conviction. Your soul has been waiting for your arrival for (what seems like) an eternity!

This is—where and how—YOU start:

Each morning, assume the position of the **HEAVEN**on**EARTH** symbol, the letter **Y.**

Your body, mind, and soul are becoming a receptive **Y.** Stretch your arms high. Reach for the sky!

The letter **Y** is the first letter of the word **Y**ES. It is also the first letter of the word **Y**OU.

Start each day by saying:

1) **Y**ES => to the goodness of heaven, pouring all its riches into **Y**OU as **Y**OU open up.
2) **Y**ES => to **Y**OUR Self, acknowledging **Y**OUR own goodness and accepting **Y**OUR worthiness.

This is how **Y**OU receive **blessings** from heaven every day,
serving **Y**OU
to personally **thrive** and generously **share** with others.

Heaven on Earth©

This is what today's **RESPONSIBILITY** exercise looks like for YOU personally:

Start by reading the RESPONSIBILITY chapter (Essential no. 5) in **GOD in a backpack** to get inspired. Then do the following exercises:

1) **Receive** responsibility. Get in touch with your natural sense of responsibility *within*. Heaven knows how to be responsible in all situations—and so do you—if you choose to live from your heart. Of course, you can only *access* heaven in your heart if you have allowed the *truth* to enter, to do its regular maintenance, keeping your heart pure and innocent. Your 3rd Essential will help you with that, should you need another "swipe of the heart" (revisit chapter TRUTH if need be).
Responsibility is an ethical and natural way of true life. Heaven does not have to *think* about being responsible; it just is. Love cares. Humans, having strayed from love, are more used to **bad** behavior than **good** behavior. This is most unfortunate because it comes with hurting self and others in the process. However, we have the power of choice! We are given *free will* and we can choose *loving kindness* instead, which always cares and is always responsible. Heaven will support us in our healthy choices, but we must invite it. Ask!
Receive heaven's guidance today, and journal about the advice it gave you. What did responsibility whisper?

2) **Be** responsibility. How can you be responsible unto your own self today? You owe yourself responsibility because this is how God originally made you. He placed a healthy conscience in you, which is your measuring stick knowing right from wrong. It actually feels good to do the right thing—much better—than to do the wrong thing. Live and observe the difference! By remembering you *are* love, you become naturally responsible and start caring for yourself, others, and our precious earth. Enjoy your responsible self :)
Write in your journal how love, responsibility, and free will are all connected. What healthy choices have you made today? The most ***important*** and most ***responsible*** choice a human being can make is to ***love***. The rest follows naturally. You will not have to remember "all the steps" of how to live your life correctly because love knows and shows the way. If you love, you can make it to heaven *blindfolded* like an innocent child.

3) **Share** responsibility. When you share your sense of responsibility with others, you become positively infectious. You will influence people by setting the tone (not in a reprimanding way, but in a commanding way) by simply sharing who you are in truth and without telling anybody what to do. You will be loved and quietly admired for being a positive force. Be a responsible friend! *Shared* responsibility is half the chore and an excellent way to live—it ensures everyone is *safe* and taken care of and nobody feels alone in the task of caring. Our beloved earth is grateful as well. She thrives when we choose to be responsible.
Share your experiences with your journal, and tell us how wonderful it is to be around responsible people. They leave an atmosphere of beauty behind. What are *you* leaving behind today? A mantra for meditation:

We are loving people by nature, and therefore, we truly care.

The outcome of caring
is a life of Heaven on Earth for all.

Your in-depth journal notes:

1) **Receive** RESPONSIBILITY

Mention three specific experiences in your practice of receiving RESPONSIBILITY today.

How did you receive / accept / understand RESPONSIBILITY? What did you do? How did you feel?

I received RESPONSIBILITY *vertically* (from heaven) by... :

....
....
....
....
....
....
....
....
....
....
....
....
....
....

I received RESPONSIBILITY *horizontally* (from people, animals, nature, life circumstances) by... :

....
....
....
....
....
....
....
....
....
....
....
....
....
....

Bravo—well done!

Your in-depth journal notes:

2) **Be** RESPONSIBILITY

Mention three specific experiences in your practice of being RESPONSIBILITY today.

How were you responsible toward your own self? What did you do? How did you feel?

....
....
....
....
....
....
....
....
....
....
....
....
....
....
....
....
....
....
....
....
....
....
....
....
....
....
....
....

Fantastic—good job!

Your in-depth journal notes:

3) **Share** RESPONSIBILITY

Mention three specific experiences in your practice of sharing RESPONSIBILITY today.

How were you sharing RESPONSIBILITY with others? How did that affect them (and you)?

Excellent! YOU are on a brave journey. I am truly proud of YOU.

Today we become experts at **WISDOM.** Here is how to:

Receive it—**Be** it—**Share** it.

Re-read this whole page. There are small differences for you to discover. It is mostly a repetition *on purpose*. This is how we best learn! We *linger* on truthful facts of life, and we *focus* on who we want to be.

* **Receive** it—**Be** it—**Share** it * is our slogan and golden thread throughout the entire Practice Book to *deeply internalize* the 10 Essentials and to make them stick to our soul.

By launching into life with one exercise page a day, we are becoming *a living embodiment* of each Essential, grooming ourselves to be successful and kindhearted **HEAVEN**on**EARTH** citizens.

Inspired by the heart, we are creating a world where everybody has a place of safety and happiness to enjoy. A vibrant human society—sharing resources and responsibilities fairly—as God intended.

This section of our instruction manual to heaven serves the purpose of *practically applying* what we have learned in the prepping portion of **GOD in a backpack.**

Without further ado, let us get started with our valuable practice called * The BEST ME that I CAN BE * Bliss is homegrown. No fertilizer necessary, just a little WISDOM.

Dive into these exercises with glee—knowing YOU are going HOME—with each step of conviction. Your soul has been waiting for your arrival for (what seems like) an eternity!

This is—where and how—YOU start:

Each morning, assume the position of the **HEAVEN**on**EARTH** symbol, the letter **Y.**

Your body, mind, and soul are becoming a receptive **Y.** Stretch your arms high. Reach for the sky!

The letter **Y** is the first letter of the word **YES**. It is also the first letter of the word **Y**OU.

Start each day by saying:

1) **Y**ES => to the goodness of heaven, pouring all its riches into **Y**OU as **Y**OU open up.
2) **Y**ES => to **Y**OUR Self, acknowledging **Y**OUR own goodness and accepting **Y**OUR worthiness.

This is how **Y**OU receive **blessings** from heaven every day,
serving **Y**OU
to personally **thrive** and generously **share** with others.

Heaven on Earth©

This is what today's **WISDOM** exercise looks like for YOU personally:

Start by re-reading the WISDOM chapter (Essential no. 6) in **GOD in a backpack** to get inspired.
Then do the following exercises:

1) **Receive** wisdom. Receiving wisdom is a gift from heaven. How can you hear and understand heavenly wisdom? You *listen* within. Make room for quiet times. Pray, meditate, relax, and trust. Give yourself a chance to get acquainted with heaven's language. Over time, you will know what voices are from heaven and what voices are distracting, disturbing *human* voices circling in your head, preventing you from peace of mind. Heaven's voice is always gentle and encouraging (except when warning you from danger!). It is never a wordy monologue without regard for your well-being. Trust yourself to be perfectly capable of differentiating between the human chatter and the heavenly voice, as they are very distinct! One is *impatient and harsh*, the other *loving and tender*. The latter is like listening to an old friend: your soul. You will recognize the true voice by how respectful, caring, and clear it is.

Living in a fast-paced society, we are either on the run or technologically preoccupied, which leaves very little room for peace and quiet. Stress robs us of adequate rest, preventing us from relaxation and inward listening. Not having cultivated the art of truthful living for a while does not mean our God-given faculties are forgotten. Our natural skills have not been erased by a magic wand. They are simply lying dormant, waiting to be re-awakened. You have the power and will to *awaken*! Claim your birthright by slowing down. Be still and discover your sweet inner peace. Heaven will reveal its wisdom as you make room for a quiet guest: your Holy Spirit. Make Him the permanent host of your soul. Climb upon your throne and rule your country—it is time to live a life of mastery—in your body, mind, and soul. As a child of God, you have been given a throne that only you can occupy. It has been waiting for its occupant for eons! This throne is *your sacred heart* at the very core of your soul, which only takes directives from your Holy Spirit. A wise and gentle voice *within*, guiding you with love.

Listen ...

Living life *fully* is another gateway to wisdom. When you surrender to life, as God created it, you can glean wisdom by completely immersing yourself. As you process your experiences and contemplate the consequences, you are able to derive deep personal wisdom. Allow yourself experiences of receiving wisdom from *heaven* and *life* itself. Listen for it, look for it, expect it, find it, feel it, be it. You cannot *miss* wisdom once you **open up** to it. Your journal pages are expecting you with great curiosity. How did wisdom direct you today?

2) **Be** wisdom. Being wise is *easy* when you love because love *is* wise. Be wise with your own self today. Watch how you treat yourself, how you take care of yourself, and how you plan for yourself. Decide what is truly in your best interest, not in a "selfish" but self-responsible way. Be your own best friend today! Celebrate your personal wisdom and apply it in your daily affairs. The **wisest** thing you can do in life is to be **kind**. Experience life from that angle today and journal accordingly. You will be very pleased with yourself.

3) **Share** wisdom. Sharing wisdom is exquisite, for yourself as well as others. True wisdom is what people are thirsty and hungry for. Our souls are parched—they *long* for wisdom of the ages—they *long* for heaven—they *long* for right and good living. We are worthy of what wisdom has to offer! Lean into your personal wisdom today, and fulfill your own longing by loving yourself. Share yourself from that place with everybody you meet. Be wise in what you say and how you say it. Your Holy Spirit will guide you. Put Him at the helm of your life! You will be smitten by your own words of wisdom streaming from your holy self onto your journal pages.

Your in-depth journal notes:

1) **Receive** WISDOM

Mention three specific experiences in your practice of receiving WISDOM today.

How did you receive WISDOM? What did you do? How did you feel?

I received WISDOM *vertically* (from heaven) by... :

....
....
....
....
....
....
....
....
....
....
....
....
....
....

I received WISDOM *horizontally* (from people, animals, nature, life circumstances) by... :

....
....
....
....
....
....
....
....
....
....
....
....
....
....

Bravo—well done!

Your in-depth journal notes:

2) **Be** WISDOM

Mention three specific experiences in your practice of being WISDOM today.

What WISDOM did you offer yourself? How did that make you feel?

....

....

....

....

....

....

....

....

....

....

....

....

....

....

....

....

....

....

....

....

....

....

....

....

....

....

....

....

....

Fantastic—good job!

Your in-depth journal notes:

3) **Share** WISDOM

Mention three specific experiences in your practice of sharing WISDOM today.

How did you share WISDOM with others? How did that affect them (and you)?

....
....
....
....
....
....
....
....
....
....
....
....
....
....
....
....
....
....
....
....
....
....
....
....
....
....
....
....
....
....
....

Excellent! YOU are on a brave journey. I am truly proud of YOU.

Today we become experts at **FORGIVENESS.** Here is how to:

Receive it—Be it—Share it.

Re-read this whole page. There are small differences for you to discover. It is mostly a repetition *on purpose*. This is how we best learn! We *linger* on truthful facts of life, and we *focus* on who we want to be.

* **Receive** it—**Be** it—**Share** it * is our slogan and golden thread throughout the entire Practice Book to *deeply internalize* the 10 Essentials and to make them stick to our soul.

By launching into life with one exercise page a day, we are becoming *a living embodiment* of each Essential, grooming ourselves to be successful and kindhearted **HEAVEN**on**EARTH** citizens.

Inspired by the heart, we are creating a world where everybody has a place of safety and happiness to enjoy. A vibrant human society—sharing resources and responsibilities fairly—as God intended.

This section of our instruction manual to heaven serves the purpose of *practically applying* what we have learned in the prepping portion of **GOD in a backpack.**

Without further ado, let us get started with our valuable practice called * The BEST ME that I CAN BE * Bliss is homegrown. No fertilizer necessary, just a little FORGIVENESS.

Dive into these exercises with glee—knowing YOU are going HOME—with each step of conviction. Your soul has been waiting for your arrival for (what seems like) an eternity!

This is—where and how—YOU start:

Each morning, assume the position of the **HEAVEN**on**EARTH** symbol, the letter **Y.**

Your body, mind, and soul are becoming a receptive **Y.** Stretch your arms high. Reach for the sky!

The letter **Y** is the first letter of the word **Y**ES. It is also the first letter of the word **Y**OU.

Start each day by saying:

1) **Y**ES => to the goodness of heaven, pouring all its riches into **Y**OU as **Y**OU open up.
2) **Y**ES => to **Y**OUR Self, acknowledging **Y**OUR own goodness and accepting **Y**OUR worthiness.

This is how **Y**OU receive **blessings** from heaven every day,
serving **Y**OU
to personally **thrive** and generously **share** with others.

Heaven on Earth©

This is what today's **FORGIVENESS** exercise looks like for YOU personally:

Start by re-reading the FORGIVENESS chapter (Essential no. 7) in **GOD in a backpack** to get inspired.
Then do the following exercises:

1) **Receive** forgiveness. Receive the grace of forgiveness, for yourself and others. This is the only way to be truly human because we are bound to make mistakes on our journey of learning how to live an ethical life. As a society, we depend on forgiveness for survival. The best place to learn mercy from is heaven. Go to your heart (heaven's earthly residence) where you fight your battles with honor. Everything in our human lives depends on our re-connection with our origin: **heaven, a place of pure love** that will lend us the necessary strength to forgive. Ask for support if you feel you cannot do it alone. Love from heaven will help you heal the wounds you thought would never heal—and shift the mountains of hurt you thought you could never climb. Forgiveness is our God-given medicine. Allow heaven to be your doctor today! Once we recognize that **all** of humanity is born in heaven, we never again hurt another person because we clearly see each other's preciousness. Journal about your personal experience of receiving forgiveness today. Describe how good it feels to be forgiven. Your soul appreciates your inward gaze.

Allow yourself the gift of mercy, and watch grace dissolve your past.

2) **Be** forgiveness by not withholding grace from anyone, not even from yourself! We are here on earth to emulate heaven, which is our springboard to right living. Heaven is our university where proficiency in ethical living is learned. No worldly school can teach us more, no matter the Ph.D.'s or certificates awarded. The greatest award anyone can earn is a great relationship with heaven. It is the purest source of information. Check in with your heart (your other heaven) and go to school there every day. It will let you know what forgiveness means and how to overcome the worst of atrocities. Forgiveness is wrenched free by the sweat of your soul. Only your soul has that much valor! Your soul is the vessel of your heart -> steer it toward freedom. Today's journal entry will be very touching. You might weep, which is OK. That is how you release hurt and how you heal. Forgive yourself and your perpetrators. The sooner you do, the less long you ache. Forgiveness is the ultimate expression of humbleness—with the power to resurrect you from the grave of your imprisoned pains.

Tread gently on your worn-out carpets of the past ... rise above them!

3) **Share** forgiveness. Once you have done battle with yourself and earned the grace of self-forgiveness, you are able to share heavenly grace with others. Forgiven people feel restored and free. You are *worth* that much and more! And so are your brothers and sisters. We forgive, not to validate wrong behavior, but to validate our soul that belongs to God. With forgiveness, we rinse off the muck to help our soul shine again, building a new life from a place of purity. Today you will feel like a phoenix rising from the ashes!

Your journal might show some tears of gladness on its pages.
Whom have you decided to forgive?

Your in-depth journal notes:

1) **Receive** FORGIVENESS

Mention three specific experiences in your practice of receiving FORGIVENESS today.

How did you receive FORGIVENESS? What were you feeling in the process?

I received FORGIVENESS *vertically* (from heaven) by… :

....
....
....
....
....
....
....
....
....
....
....
....
....
....

I received FORGIVENESS *horizontally* (from people, animals, nature, life circumstances) by… :

....
....
....
....
....
....
....
....
....
....
....
....
....
....

Bravo—well done!

Your in-depth journal notes:

2) **Be** FORGIVENESS

Mention three specific experiences in your practice of being FORGIVENESS today.

How did you forgive yourself? How did that make you feel?

....
....
....
....
....
....
....
....
....
....
....
....
....
....
....
....
....
....
....
....
....
....
....
....
....
....
....
....
....
....

Fantastic—good job!

Your in-depth journal notes:

3) **Share** FORGIVENESS

Mention <u>three specific experiences</u> in your practice of <u>sharing FORGIVENESS</u> today.

Whom or what did you forgive? What feelings did your FORGIVENESS provoke? What changed?

....
....
....
....
....
....
....
....
....
....
....
....
....
....
....
....
....
....
....
....
....
....
....
....
....
....
....
....
....
....
....
....
....

Excellent! YOU are on a brave journey. I am truly proud of YOU.

Today we become experts at **HUMOR.** Here is how to:

Receive it—**Be** it—**Share** it.

Re-read this whole page. There are small differences for you to discover. It is mostly a repetition *on purpose.*
This is how we best learn! We *linger* on truthful facts of life, and we *focus* on who we want to be.

* **Receive** it—**Be** it—**Share** it * is our slogan and golden thread throughout the entire Practice Book
to *deeply internalize* the 10 Essentials and to make them stick to our soul.

By launching into life with one exercise page a day, we are becoming *a living embodiment* of each Essential,
grooming ourselves to be successful and kindhearted **HEAVEN**on**EARTH** citizens.

Inspired by the heart, we are creating a world where everybody has a place of safety and happiness to enjoy.
A vibrant human society—sharing resources and responsibilities fairly—as God intended.

This section of our instruction manual to heaven serves the purpose of *practically applying*
what we have learned in the prepping portion of **GOD in a backpack.**

Without further ado, let us get started with our valuable practice called * The BEST ME that I CAN BE *
Bliss is homegrown. No fertilizer necessary, just a little HUMOR.

Dive into these exercises with glee—knowing YOU are going HOME—with each step of conviction.
Your soul has been waiting for your arrival for (what seems like) an eternity!

This is—where and how—YOU start:

Each morning, assume the position of the **HEAVEN**on**EARTH** symbol, the letter **Y.**

Your body, mind, and soul are becoming a receptive **Y.** Stretch your arms high. Reach for the sky!

The letter **Y** is the first letter of the word **Y**ES. It is also the first letter of the word **Y**OU.

Start each day by saying:

1) **Y**ES => to the goodness of heaven, pouring all its riches into **Y**OU as **Y**OU open up.
2) **Y**ES => to **Y**OUR Self, acknowledging **Y**OUR own goodness and accepting **Y**OUR worthiness.

This is how **Y**OU receive **blessings** from heaven every day,
serving **Y**OU
to personally **thrive** and generously **share** with others.

This is what today's **HUMOR** exercise looks like for YOU personally:

Start by re-reading the HUMOR chapter (Essential no. 8) in **GOD in a backpack** to get inspired.
Then do the following exercises:

1) **Receive** humor. Humor is a delightful gift. It makes everyone feel light and *see* the light (truth). Today we are going to laugh about the funny behavior of *looking* for the *obvious*. Let us start with the example of a man looking for his glasses while he is wearing them on his nose all along. Next, picture a dog chasing her tail, thinking she is chasing after a creature other than herself. Now, imagine a fish looking for water. Are you chuckling yet? Hold your breath—it is going to get funnier: Have you heard of humans *looking* for God? Why and how is that funny? Because God is <u>omnipresent</u>, meaning everywhere, which *includes* you and me! Why *look* for God? Find humor in the compulsive human search of *looking* for the *obvious* presence of God (of which our breath and heartbeat are proof, they are clearly not factory-made)! How much more *obvious* can God possibly be? <u>God lives **in us** and **through us** as the **breath of life**</u>. Why *look* beyond ourselves?

Today you are invited to crack the seal of ignorance with goodhearted laughter! Together we can turn our human dilemma into human grace by simply laughing out loud at ourselves. Apply the medicine of self-effacing humor: Look into the mirror until you laugh, then wipe your tears of inner release, washing away your blindness for good! Keep looking into the mirror and observe gladness, relief, understanding, and forgiveness surface in your eyes. Now, thank humor for being your band-aid *and* life coach today!
Your journal notes will be lighthearted and spiked with the *epiphany* of God being "as close as your nose."

2) **Be** humor. Humor is a lighthearted ... feather in a storm ... and an amusing companion. When hiking, and you happen to fall flat on your face into a puddle of mud, humor can come in handy! Here are a couple of jokes to counterbalance such "tragedies" and to practice a light heart :)

    Joke no. 1) Why did God create eternity?
                  He knew it would take us—a while—to figure life out.
    Joke no. 2) A foreign exchange student asks her language teacher:
                  Why do you say in English: The alarm goes **OFF** when it goes **ON** ... waking me up?
    Joke no. 3) How do you make holy water?
                  You boil the living hell out of it!
    Joke no. 4) This one is on you :)

Your task today is to find your *own* funny streak within. Describe in your journal how you unearthed humor for yourself. You will most certainly fall asleep with a light heart.

3) **Share** humor. Why? I have little of it as is! Don't worry. Once you start sharing humor, it multiplies. One of the greatest gifts you will ever share with another human being is humor. Laughing *with* someone creates some of the best memories of your life. What memories have *you* created today? Your journal will reveal how humor has healed your soul and the soul of others. Thank you for carrying us through the valleys of darkness with the lightness of your spirit! You made me smile and fly ... I hardly even touched the ground.

See you in heaven—I have a gift of gratitude waiting for you!

Your in-depth journal notes:

1) **Receive** HUMOR

Mention three specific experiences in your practice of receiving HUMOR today.

How did you receive HUMOR? What did you do? How did you feel?

I received HUMOR *vertically* (from heaven) by... :

....
....
....
....
....
....
....
....
....
....
....
....
....
....

I received HUMOR *horizontally* (from people, animals, nature, life circumstances) by... :

....
....
....
....
....
....
....
....
....
....
....
....
....
....

Bravo—well done!

Your in-depth journal notes:

2) **Be** HUMOR

Mention three specific experiences in your practice of being HUMOR today.

In what way were you—humorous and lighthearted—with your own self? How did that make you feel?

....
....
....
....
....
....
....
....
....
....
....
....
....
....
....
....
....
....
....
....
....
....
....
....
....
....
....
....

Fantastic—good job!

Your in-depth journal notes:

3) **Share** HUMOR

Mention <u>three specific experiences</u> in your practice of <u>sharing HUMOR</u> today.

How did you share HUMOR with others? How did that affect them (and you)?

....
....
....
....
....
....
....
....
....
....
....
....
....
....
....
....
....
....
....
....
....
....
....
....
....
....
....
....

Excellent! YOU are on a brave journey. I am truly proud of YOU.

Today we become experts at **ART.** Here is how to:

Receive it—**Be** it—**Share** it.

Re-read this whole page. There are small differences for you to discover. It is mostly a repetition *on purpose.* This is how we best learn! We *linger* on truthful facts of life, and we *focus* on who we want to be.

* **Receive** it—**Be** it—**Share** it * is our slogan and golden thread throughout the entire Practice Book to *deeply internalize* the 10 Essentials and to make them stick to our soul.

By launching into life with one exercise page a day, we are becoming *a living embodiment* of each Essential, grooming ourselves to be successful and kindhearted **HEAVEN**on**EARTH** citizens.

Inspired by the heart, we are creating a world where everybody has a place of safety and happiness to enjoy. A vibrant human society—sharing resources and responsibilities fairly—as God intended.

This section of our instruction manual to heaven serves the purpose of *practically applying* what we have learned in the prepping portion of **GOD in a backpack.**

Without further ado, let us get started with our valuable practice called * The BEST ME that I CAN BE * Bliss is homegrown. No fertilizer necessary, just a little ART.

Dive into these exercises with glee—knowing YOU are going HOME—with each step of conviction. Your soul has been waiting for your arrival for (what seems like) an eternity!

This is—where and how—YOU start:

Each morning, assume the position of the **HEAVEN**on**EARTH** symbol, the letter **Y.**

Your body, mind, and soul are becoming a receptive **Y.** Stretch your arms high. Reach for the sky!

The letter **Y** is the first letter of the word **Y**ES. It is also the first letter of the word **Y**OU.

Start each day by saying:

1) **Y**ES => to the goodness of heaven, pouring all its riches into **Y**OU as **Y**OU open up.
2) **Y**ES => to **Y**OUR Self, acknowledging **Y**OUR own goodness and accepting **Y**OUR worthiness.

This is how **Y**OU receive **blessings** from heaven every day,
serving **Y**OU
to personally **thrive** and generously **share** with others.

Heaven on Earth©

This is what today's **ART** exercise looks like for YOU personally:

Start by re-reading the ART chapter (Essential no. 9) in **GOD in a backpack** to get inspired.
Then do the following exercises:

1) **Receive** art. God created all things so very beautiful, and believe it or not, that includes YOU.
Do you love the beauty of our universe? Take it in. Be mesmerized! Do you love the beauty of YOU?
Learn to appreciate yourself equally. Once you find true beauty in yourself, you are able to find authentic
beauty in others. Today's exercise is no beauty contest, no egotistical self-adoration, but a practice to see
yourself as God sees you, from the inside out. Drop all self-criticism. Together we are practicing self-honor.
Once that is established, our eyes are more apt to see beauty all around us, and we start *caring* for our
magnificent planet earth and each other. Allow nature to nourish you with its daily art display!
Receive art in your heart today, and journal like a breath of fresh air ...

2) **Be** art. Breathe and feel your cells. Your body is a grand design of harmonious patterns, all interacting and
moving. Feel your aliveness! Look at the ART in YOU (in front of a mirror) and look with eyes of tolerance and
kindness. The way God made you is perfect. Nobody looks like you, and that is a miracle. God adores you with
every hair, crooked or not. When you look at yourself today, discover your favorite ART sculpture called SELF.
Observe and feel your touch, your skin, your breath, your eyes. Oh my, I shiver at your sight—I see your light!
A sculpture may be beautiful but will never *breathe* like you. Offer yourself beauty today. Perhaps you love
flowers? Perhaps you feel artful through sports, being engaged in the beauty of movement? If you do not feel
athletic or artful, you can always practice. Find personal grace. Pay attention *how* you roll your foot ... and tread
kindly, life is an artful walk. If you are not able to walk, practice a graceful hand movement or simply smile!
Choose to *glow* today and do what makes you feel beautiful. This day is your opportunity to fall in love with
yourself all over again or perhaps for the first time?

Journal with grace.

3) **Share** art. Be yourself today (which is true art) and share your natural self with others. Practice being truly
comfortable in your skin and proud of who you are without being prideful. The best people to meet are the ones
who have completely accepted themselves (perfect or not) and who carry their natural beauty without
the slightest hint of vanity. That is art well shared. While assuming a graceful body posture today (to practice art),
look at others with a kind eye. They are "art on the go" ... shopping, walking, conversing, breathing.
Everybody is God's creation, unendingly ravishing and simply striking, even in their oddness. Fall in love with
every look, race, age, and shape because—in God's eyes—we all are "art in motion" and truly irresistible to Him!
How about we treat each other from His vantage point? When you meet people today who do not feel so good
about themselves, be *you* their admirer and best witness. See them through God's eyes.
Journal how good it feels to share art and grace with others. Learn the art of uplifting companionship.

You are inspiring! Thank you for seeing beauty in me.

Your in-depth journal notes:

1) **Receive** ART

Mention three specific experiences in your practice of receiving ART today.

How did you receive ART? What did you do? What feelings emerged?

I received ART *vertically* (from heaven) by... :

....
....
....
....
....
....
....
....
....
....
....
....
....

I received ART *horizontally* (from people, animals, nature, life circumstances) by... :

....
....
....
....
....
....
....
....
....
....
....
....

Bravo—well done!

Your in-depth journal notes:

2) **Be** ART

Mention three specific experiences in your practice of being ART today.

How did you celebrate your artful self? How did that make you feel?

....
....
....
....
....
....
....
....
....
....
....
....
....
....
....
....
....
....
....
....
....
....
....
....
....
....
....
....

Fantastic—good job!

Your in-depth journal notes:

3) **Share** ART

Mention three specific experiences in your practice of sharing ART today.

How did you share ART with others? How did that affect them (and you)?

....
....
....
....
....
....
....
....
....
....
....
....
....
....
....
....
....
....
....
....
....
....
....
....
....
....
....
....
....
....

Excellent! YOU are on a brave journey. I am truly proud of YOU.

Today we become experts at **SIMPLICITY.** Here is how to:

Receive it—**Be** it—**Share** it.

Re-read this whole page. There are small differences for you to discover. It is mostly a repetition *on purpose.* This is how we best learn! We *linger* on truthful facts of life, and we *focus* on who we want to be.

* **Receive** it—**Be** it—**Share** it * is our slogan and golden thread throughout the entire Practice Book to *deeply internalize* the 10 Essentials and to make them stick to our soul.

By launching into life with one exercise page a day, we are becoming *a living embodiment* of each Essential, grooming ourselves to be successful and kindhearted **HEAVEN**on**EARTH** citizens.

Inspired by the heart, we are creating a world where everybody has a place of safety and happiness to enjoy. A vibrant human society—sharing resources and responsibilities fairly—as God intended.

This section of our instruction manual to heaven serves the purpose of *practically applying* what we have learned in the prepping portion of **GOD in a backpack.**

Without further ado, let us get started with our valuable practice called * The BEST ME that I CAN BE * Bliss is homegrown. No fertilizer necessary, just a little SIMPLICITY.

Dive into these exercises with glee—knowing YOU are going HOME—with each step of conviction. Your soul has been waiting for your arrival for (what seems like) an eternity!

This is—where and how—YOU start:

Each morning, assume the position of the **HEAVEN**on**EARTH** symbol, the letter **Y.**

Your body, mind, and soul are becoming a receptive **Y.** Stretch your arms high. Reach for the sky!

The letter **Y** is the first letter of the word **YES.** It is also the first letter of the word **YOU.**

Start each day by saying:

1) **Y**ES => to the goodness of heaven, pouring all its riches into **YOU** as **YOU** open up.
2) **Y**ES => to **Y**OUR Self, acknowledging **Y**OUR own goodness and accepting **Y**OUR worthiness.

This is how **YOU** receive **blessings** from heaven every day,
serving **YOU**
to personally **thrive** and generously **share** with others.

Heaven on Earth©

This is what today's **SIMPLICITY** exercise looks like for YOU personally:

Start by re-reading the SIMPLICITY chapter (Essential no. 10) in **GOD in a backpack** to get inspired.
Then do the following exercises:

1) **Receive** simplicity. *Receive love.*

Receive God's gift of simplicity. He placed Himself in your heart!
Open the present. *Open* your heart.

His love is your providence.
Seek you the Kingdom of Heaven first (**love within**) and all else shall be **added** unto you.
That is His promise to you!
Experiment with it.

Meditate on the above, and fill your journal with simple solutions.
Could it be as easy as being *open*?

2) **Be** simplicity. *Be love.*

As a sunray is connected to the sun, YOU are connected to the origin of LOVE. Love is your *nature,* and you are heaven's extension. Be the sunray you are born to be! Shine and love. Does a sunray ever worry about light? Neither shall you worry about love. Love is issued from heaven and flows through you as *naturally* as the sunlight flows from the sun into each ray. <u>Simply be YOU.</u> Journal how much easier life is, not wanting to be anything or anyone else. Knowing you were handcrafted by God in heaven, makes you a *quality* product of love! You can trust yourself fully. Feel into your loving self today and experience God from a personal angle. Notice how **simple** it is to access our Creator by contacting your own heart. What could be more comforting than a regular heartbeat, reassuring you, He is with you every step of the way?

Love is **simple** because God built you (not with bricks … but) with His eternal love.
You are His arms, His eyes, His ears on the ground!

3) **Share** simplicity. *Extend love.*

You have **found** the Kingdom of Heaven (**within your loving heart**). This is **your** Heaven on Earth.
There is nothing more precious to share!
Pay attention, as you journal, how love wants to simply be *lived* and how *you* can fulfill its wish.

It is as simple as … **being** … as God made you.

You are a body of **LOVE** … walk it out !

Your in-depth journal notes:

1) **Receive** SIMPLICITY

Mention three specific experiences in your practice of receiving SIMPLICITY today.

How did you receive SIMPLICITY? What did you do? How did you feel?

I received SIMPLICITY *vertically* (from heaven) by... :

....

....

....

....

....

....

....

....

....

....

....

....

I received SIMPLICITY *horizontally* (from people, animals, nature, life circumstances) by... :

....

....

....

....

....

....

....

....

....

....

....

....

Bravo—well done!

Your in-depth journal notes:

2) **Be** SIMPLICITY

Mention <u>three specific experiences</u> in your practice of <u>being SIMPLICITY</u> today.

How did you simplify your life? How did it *feel* to simply *be*?

....
....
....
....
....
....
....
....
....
....
....
....
....
....
....
....
....
....
....
....
....
....
....
....
....
....
....
....
....

Fantastic—good job!

Your in-depth journal notes:

3) **Share** SIMPLICITY

Mention three specific experiences in your practice of sharing SIMPLICITY today.

How did you share SIMPLICITY with others? How did that make them (and you) feel?

....
....
....
....
....
....
....
....
....
....
....
....
....
....
....
....
....
....
....
....
....
....
....
....
....
....
....
....
....
....

Excellent! YOU are on a brave journey. I am truly proud of YOU.

You have come to a **GLORIOUS END** of your Practice Book, with lots of beautiful notes to share. Bravo! Treat this journal as precious gold. The GOLD you found in YOU. It reflects your many breakthroughs and insights. Take a moment to celebrate your profound understanding. Upon re-visiting your notes at a later date, you will be stunned at how much you have learned, better yet *remembered*. You now know yourself.

Peace is yours forever ...

I recommend you date your entries. For best results, allocate one month for the Practice Book. Science says, by day 21, you will have built new habits that stick. That is our goal. If you take three days per Essential, doing one exercise page a day, you will see a new life emerge before your very eyes. Observe your growth!

Your **10 Essentials** are now your integrated **HEAVEN**on**EARTH** habits.

They represent **GOD**—they represent **LOVE**—they represent **YOU**.
What a beautiful person you are!

How does it feel to be your newly *realized* **YOU**?
A **YOU**—you have always been—but never *really* knew?

The tremendous **GIFT** you have **accepted** by saying **YES** to a journey of self-discovery
... keeps on giving ...

Before diving back into the world,
which you now walk with confidence and knowingness,
I am seeing you off with an Appendix that brings it all HOME.

It is called

The **SOLUTION.**

Consider it a bonus for all your good work!

Its genre is similar, yet different
and even though not directly related to **GOD in a backpack**,
it makes for a perfect finish.

*Imagine taking off your backpack ...
... sitting by the campfire
and sharing this last story with one another ...*

Part III   Appendix:
The **SOLUTION**

The next few pages talk about a Linchpin.

What is a Linchpin?

A crucial piece that holds it all together.

The word originated in the 14th century and was more known during the wild west of North America when wagons ventured west to live a life of freedom. Each wagon wheel was fastened to the axle via a Linchpin, without which the whole wagon would fall apart (imagine a strong **U**-shaped metal pin, squeezed together at the center of the wheel to prevent it from slipping off the axle).

Nowadays, the term is used more symbolically, signifying high importance or central station because everything hinges upon it.

What is fascinating about the word is the fact that it is a "tiny but pivotal" part of the whole, without which nothing works.

The same is true about **ONE** human being, apparently insignificant in the scope of the grandeur of existence. Yet, each person holds the power to create (or destroy).

As **EACH** cell matters in a human body, **YOU** matter in life and can make all the difference!

YOU
... are the crown jewel of creation, the pinnacle, pride and joy of God.
In His eyes, you are royalty, and as such, you are given a throne:
your heart.

When you act from your heart ...

YOU
become
The **SOLUTION.**

The Linchpin of Life

Have you ever had deep questions and thought you will probably never find all the answers?
Even if you dedicated your whole life researching the truth in all earnestness?

You are not alone. Humanity has been plagued with myriads of questions and less than satisfying answers ever since the beginning of time.

Today we explore a Revelation of the Soul that shall offer you relief from ancient human agony.
In its application lies the prize! Refreshingly so, it is easy and natural. Nobody is above or beneath its reach.
It is The **Answer** we have all been looking for.

The Linchpin of Life shines a light through the cobwebs of complexity. Your eyes will see anew, and your mind will be humbled by the Reality of Simplicity. You will be **free** forever and never again left without an answer.
Henceforth, you will know <u>what to do</u> when something is amiss and <u>how to be</u>.

That is the promise.

For starters, we shall glance over a list of ancient human questions together …

What is the purpose of humankind?

What is my purpose?

What is the will of God?

What is the truth?

What is life all about?

What is life made of?

Where do I come from?

Where do I go to?

Who am I?

Who is God? What is God?

What stands behind creation—even if I refuse to believe in God?

What brings joy without fail?

What created light, and what generates more light?

What is the greatest power on earth or in the universe(s)?

What matters the most?

What makes our heart sing?

What are we most yearning for as humans?

What is of greatest value?

What should we focus on? What instills the will to live?

What makes others (humans, animals, plants) **feel best?**

What makes the greatest difference?

What quality of life changes everything?

What is most important to know?

What is most important to learn or instill?

What is the holy grail? Where is it to be found?

Am I in truth the very thing (_____) that I once thought I needed to learn?
put your answer here

Many philosophers, scientists, and theologians have pondered similar questions for eons. Innumerable volumes have been written—and hundreds of libraries have been filled—with as many questions and answers as diverging points of view.

What can we all agree on? Is there a truth that pulls us all together?

In the midst of such contemplation, **ONE** answer suddenly emerges as the perfect fit for all the questions humanity has ever asked.

With the gentleness of a butterfly, this graceful answer softly lands on my heart, leaving an unforgettable imprint of ...

KINDNESS.

A coin drops.
Stillness is all I hear.
This quiet revelation of KINDNESS slowly settles into my fibers, instilling a sense of wonder.

How can **ONE** word offer such grace as to solve all ancient riddles at once—freeing humanity from painful confusion and complexity? A word with the power of dissolving separation into unity?

I allow my mind the time it takes to grapple with a solution so *simple* by scanning over the list of questions, again and again, arriving at the same result. KINDNESS fits as an answer in each case! How profound and mesmerizing. Happily exhausted, I surrender my struggle and allow the **truth** to sink in.

It issues a clear directive:

A word alone is mere theory. The day it becomes your action, you become a hero!

Make Kindness your Lifestyle.

It is time to put our Linchpin to work. After reading this document, you will have the opportunity to personalize your experience with KINDNESS by going over each question yourself. You will be amazed.

Next, apply KINDNESS pertaining to your own questions. Either the word KINDNESS fits as an answer or the *approach* of KINDNESS will. If you ask, for example: Why is there misery? The *lack* of KINDNESS is the answer. However, you also have an immediate solution at hand: Be kind to fix the problem!

Or you might wonder—is there a heaven or a hell? Where there is KINDNESS, there is heaven. Where there is a *lack* of KINDNESS, there is hell. Heaven is omnipresent (like love) and has not gone anywhere. We just overlaid it with lies, corruption, and complexity (the dark clouds in the sky). Acts of KINDNESS lift the fog and shift the clouds until our blue sky reappears!

That is Heaven on Earth.

By adopting KINDNESS as the remedy for all ills and answer to all questions, your life becomes focused on where the greatest **power** lies. With repeated practice and application, you will discover that all of life, its challenges *and* solutions **revolve** around KINDNESS. KINDNESS truly is The **Answer** to the crux of life! Why fix a hole with chewing gum, which sooner or later becomes brittle, falls off, and recreates the problem ... when KINDNESS offers the *permanent* solution and fixes the hole for good?

Humanity has many such holes that can be fixed with KINDNESS.

When engaged in your own question & answer process (later on), you may substitute the word KINDNESS with the word LOVE where it seems a better fit. Play with both terms and interchange them freely. LOVE always makes sense, of course, and will bring the same results in your experiment. KINDNESS is simply an easier word and less subject to misinterpretation. Everybody instantly knows what "kind" means.

This makes KINDNESS our perfect Linchpin!

Let us move to the exercise part for you to verify that KINDNESS works without exception.
We will do a couple of test questions together to give you a taste of our Linchpin in action. You will soon discover how far-reaching KINDNESS really is. It is applicable in every life scenario, seen and unseen. Creation itself was born in the womb of KINDNESS, which later birthed us! Being kind is our very nature. Being **un**kind is **un**natural. When **un**kind, we are acting like strangers in our own homeland.

Are you ready to turn **the master key** KINDNESS and open some doors you thought forever shut?
See for yourself whether it fits into the keyhole of the first three doors (questions) that follow:

OK ->   Question # 1   **What is the purpose of humankind?**

The answer is hidden (or obvious) in the title of our name: Human**kind** is supposed to be human and **kind**. KINDNESS is its purpose! The answer KINDNESS fits, does it not?

OK ->   Question # 2   **What is my purpose?**

To be kind. Again, KINDNESS fits perfectly as an answer! Do not be distraught by believing you have not discovered your purpose yet—since KINDNESS is a *quality* and therefore *applicable* in any circumstance of life. As long as you are *kind* and are doing whatever you call your profession or task *with* KINDNESS, you cannot possibly miss your purpose—and you will have fulfilled the will of God!

This leads us to our last question (below) before you are off on your own having fun with the exercise. While weighing each question against a feather (… kindness …) you will soon enough experience the enormity of the word, observe its tremendous outreach, and discover its power and delightful simplicity.

OK ->   Question # 3   **What is the will of God?**

KINDNESS. One more time, the answer is a perfect fit! We often imagine in our immaturity as humans, the will of God to be larger than life, impossible to know, let alone fulfill. That is simply not true. Not only is God very accessible, He is ONE with us through LOVE and **wills** nothing but **KINDNESS** for us all.

Being kind is very doable, is it not?

Sometimes, it just takes a smile—where language, culture, or religion are a barrier. KINDNESS is the glue that makes us **ONE**. See how simple life gets once you know the truth? The way to measure truth is by asking yourself—does it apply to all people, to all of life, consistently so? If it is inclusive and consistent, it is the truth.

A genuine smile and KINDNESS are universally applicable and the easiest, most natural expressions of truth. Where words and holy books may clash, **kind gestures** have the capacity to stretch themselves across the globe and reach every single soul.

☺ Put KINDNESS to the test ☺
You cannot possibly fail—and it will never fail you.

With your participation, we can all re-establish our lost paradise and live a life of Heaven on Earth. It is as easy as being kind!

Kindness is the Linchpin of Life.

Now, you may go back to the list of questions and continue testing KINDNESS as the ideal answer. Enjoy the experience of holding **the master key** in your hands with the **power** of solving all of the world's riddles and problems at once. Turn the key … and the world will turn in the direction of your heart's desire!

Dear Readers, we are herewith rapidly approaching the end of our entire book.

Now that you are holding
The **MASTER KEY**
in your hands
and are in possession of
The **TRUTH** and The **SOLUTION**

... how are you going to live your life henceforth?

JUST BE KIND
one day at a time!

Create a **KINDNESS** calendar.
Buy the prettiest calendar in town—or handcraft it—then simply mark each day with a ...

smiley face

... when you have done a **KIND** act, or thought a **KIND** thought, or offered a **KIND** smile.
It feels very good to look back over your calendar each month and find a rich collection of smiles :)

These are

YOUR **PEARLS.**

Count them,   each one is

a piece of

HEAVEN on EARTH

YOU
have created!

★

You are truly
amazing.

The END

or is it a New Beginning?

With your treasure chest full to the brim

you may happily go your way

sharing your gems

with whomever

crosses your path.

May others be as **loved** by you as you are **loved** by them.

HEAVEN on EARTH

is

now YOUR new

reality.

What a wonderful world!

Lucia Elisabeth Herger is originally from Switzerland and now resides in the USA, in Washington State. She has traveled the world extensively, speaks several languages, loves nature, dance, art, and God. The Holy Spirit is her protector and mentor, direct life experience her teacher, and love her compass.

Lucia's specific niche in spiritual education is to make God easily accessible by simplifying complexity. This book is an example of her skill of squeezing the essence out of the divine. In interactive, dynamic workshops, Lucia offers experiential opportunities for people to fall in love with their own spirit.

There was a time where mind over matter was the right call. Now we have shifted into a **new era** that requires heart over mind.

This calls us to a higher standard of accepting and expressing ourselves as love—living from the **heart**—and allowing it to guide our mind, which is a giant evolutionary step humanity as a whole is on the verge of taking.

Intuitively we know, the way of the heart is the only way our earth and society will go from barely surviving to globally thriving. We have reached a critical turning point and cannot afford to linger in the outdated realm of calculated and greedy minds, looking for personal benefit only. We need to take care of the planet and each other. Our heart knows perfectly well how to do that. Trust it. It is infinitely wise.

As a certified **Encouragement Trainer**, Lucia helps people believe in themselves. She invites participants to shine their light and give their own divinity expression. Her techniques draw forth a person's greatest capacity. Lucia's present focus is to educate people to become Heaven on Earth citizens, creating a society of awakened human beings sharing kindness and celebrating joy. Imagine yourself in a dance class. You are learning the graceful steps of how to play an ethical part in the ultimate dance of life.

Enjoy the book and **share** your journey with others. Pretty soon **we are** the world we most desire!

Copyright © 2021 Lucia E Herger-Sutter

LifeRich Publishing is a registered trademark of The Reader's Digest Association, Inc.

Any people depicted in stock imagery provided by Getty Images are models, and such images are being used for illustrative purposes only. Certain stock imagery © Getty Images.

LifeRich Publishing books may be ordered through booksellers
(amazon.com, barnesandnoble.com, etc.)

or

by contacting

(USA +1) **844-686-9607**
www.liferichpublishing.com
(click on bookstore)

Write a review to the publisher to inspire others with your Heaven on Earth journey.

Library of Congress Control Number: 2019931554

ISBN: 978-1-4897-2096-2 (softcover)
ISBN: 978-1-4897-2095-5 (hardcover)
ISBN: 978-1-4897-2094-8 (e-book)
ISBN: 978-1-4897-3287-3 (audiobook)

LifeRich Publishing rev. date: 8 / 22 / 2021